Chorus

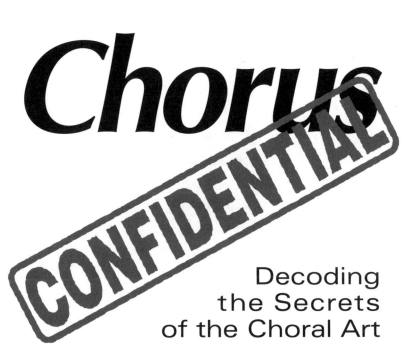

Decoding the Secrets of the Choral Art

William Dehning

Pavane Publishing

www.PavanePublishing.com

Pavane Publishing Catalog No. P5013
Hal Leonard Catalog No. 08301689
ISBN 0-634-05843-6

For my students; all thirty-seven years' worth.
I hope I haunt them.

"You don't need that."
                    —Hazel Dehning (author's mother, 1942-56)

"Who duss he think *he* iss, anawayss?"
                    —Sigurd Swanson (author's uncle, 1952-56)

" . . .they cost more. You don't need Levi's, Wranglers are just as good."
                    —Wilfred Dehning (author's father, 1956-58)

"Heck yes, go."
                    —Margaret Dehning (author's wife, 2002)

"You earned it, Papa, and it shows real *huevos*."
                    —Megan Dehning (author's daughter, 2002)

"Rock on, Dad."
                    —Elizabeth Miller (author's daughter, 2002)

"Working on a new language is good for your aging brain."
                    —Lee Miller (author's son-in-law, 2002)

TABLE OF CONTENTS

Preface

The "Leviticus" in the inception of this book (you need to wait a bit for Genesis and Exodus) came when I was standing in the outer office at U.S.C. talking to Alice Patterson one mid-afternoon in late January. Alice is the Administrator for our department. I was mewling about some problem or other and she got tired of it and said, "Why don't you take a sabbatical?" "Come to think of it," I said, "it's been fourteen years since my last one, ten of them here."

She just looked at me.

I turned on my heel instantly and squeaked along the polished waxed floor of the hall in my Old Codger sensible shoes, sounding for all the world like a hospital orderly fetching equipment for ICU, arriving at the Assistant Dean's office.

— "Susan. Is it too late to apply for a sabbatical next year?"
— "Nope." She whips out the form, handing it to me. "What are you going to do with it?"
— "I don't know. Go to Spain and write my memoirs, maybe."
— "You're too young for that."
— "I turn sixty next summer."
— "Get outta here."

Meaning by that, not, "leave my office instantly," but, "I don't believe you're going to be sixty." The flattering implication could have been that I didn't look sixty; the unflattering one, knowing me as she does, that I don't act my age and haven't grown up yet. I didn't know which inference to draw from her response and was not about to ask. I squeaked back to my office and filled out the form on the spot. Two days later, I got the green light from Susan and - zip - just like that, Alice would be rid of her Resident Jeremiah for awhile. I also got permission from my wife, whose school can't move as quickly with such things as U.S.C. can, so she would have to work while I was home alone, writing and cooking the occasional meal for us. She even let me come here alone to Spain, where I do much the same thing, except much more writing and no cooking at all.

A Market?

The pages of inception had leafed over to Exodus a couple of years ago, when Allan Petker, Director of Publications for Gentry Publications, sent me a letter out of the blue wondering if they could publish a William Dehning Choral Series. He had heard the U.S.C. Chamber Choir in San Antonio and thought the time might be ripe to capitalize on the nice, clean splash they made.

I said to him, "Thanks, but I'm a performer, not an editor or scholar; I keep my interpretations to myself until you hear them live and on stage."
— "Can we at least have lunch? Talk about it?"
— "Of course, you're very kind."

I thanked him, met with the wonderful people of the Gentry Board, agreed to a contract with no specific schedule, had a terrific lunch, and left.

And did nothing. For months. Until I had filled out the sabbatical form mentioned above, whereupon I called him.

"Allan, look, this profession does not need another Choral Series, least of all one with my name on it, a name that's neither famous nor euphonious nor pretty in print. Besides, I would consider it a simple exercise in vanity. I wouldn't be having any fun either, and if it ain't fun, why do it?"

"OK, do you want to cancel, or do you have something else in mind?"

"How about a book? One that covers the outline of my choral development class–because there is no one book that currently does–but also including most other aspects of this profession? My students have been asking for one for years. You know, a Most-Things-You-Might-Want-to-Know book about choral music making, but all in one place. Except the literature. Let's leave that to the real scholars like Nick Strimple, Lawrence Schenbeck, Gordon Paine. I think it might be more useful than a William Dehning Choral Series."

"Fine," he said, "but can it also be geared to me and my church choir, to anyone who enjoys this work...not so, you know, academic?"

"My pleasure," I said.

The Genesis of this book, then, came shuffling down hallways over many years from students in my Choral Development and conducting classes, who at the end of a semester have frequently and flatteringly (because the final exam is imminent, possibly) said, "You should write a book, Dr. Dehning."

"Pshaw," I said, for reasons already explained, "there are plenty of books out there on these topics. Look in the bibliography of the syllabus if you want more than you've already read in the course. You know what I think about it all because I told you in class...at great length. What makes you think anybody else needs to hear what I have to say?"

"Well, it's very direct, and sometimes you're funny when you say it. Even your digressions. Sometimes especially your digressions."

"Oh."

So I had permission, publisher and purpose. All I needed to do now was follow along with my notes and digress a bit apparently, and be funny while doing it. Easy enough, except for the funny part. I can only do that by accident, I think, whilst in the process of something else. Anything. I'm no stand-up comic. Intentionally, anyway.

My Story

Then last summer our friend Paul Fairbrook showed us a biography that he had done for his family. It was fascinating. My wife thought I should do something similar for our girls (even if they might not read it until I was dead) because she honestly feels that I had an interesting boyhood and did quite well for myself in most ways, given the circumstances. I pshawed that as I pshaw most such personal things at first, considering them self-indulgent or self-obsessed, and not wanting to publicly demonstrate the fact that I am both in all likelihood. Vain, too.

But as is often the case when my wife suggests something, I didn't respond right away (this drives her nuts, poor woman; she is truly the better half of this societal corporation). I did let it simmer in the garlic and oil of the present project for a month, and then when I started to finally cook — to write — at the beginning of September, I tossed her idea insouciantly into the pan and threw in a few things about my youth. She doesn't know that yet.

My daughter Elizabeth does, because I sent her the first draft of the first three chapters. I did that because a while back I asked her to be the editor. She has wonderful credentials for the job: degrees in literature, a job teaching college English, choral experience all through high school — including All-States — and college, a cello player, an incipient desire to tell her old man what to do, sired by one skinny, remarkably capable, erudite Midwestern man and married to another.

Just before I got on the plane for Spain, she called me with her reaction:

— "It's good, Dad."
— "Really?"
— "Yeah."
— "*Nun, keine Scheisse? Wirklich?*" (Her German is even better than mine).
— "*Keine Scheisse, papi.*"
— "Tell what you like."
— "Well, all of it, but do you know what I really think works?"
— "What?"

— "The autobiographical stuff, it really adds punch, makes
your points."
— "Really?! I was worried about that, ready to dump it if you
said so."
— "Keep it in, Dad."

There, you see? I didn't ask, she volunteered it. Maxwell Perkins
gives good advice to Thomas Wolfe and you are thereby stuck with the
memoir-ish quality of this book. Alone, I may have been off base to
want to use such stuff but two Dehnings can't be wrong.

Now don't fret. Most of the enthralling bi-Dehning-approved memoir
fragments are easily identified by parentheses at the end of a paragraph.
Some have warning labels; others sneak up on you. No matter, you can
skip them all if you want. Up to you. Former students and singers will
find them illuminating because they've never heard them before. In
class and rehearsal, I'm all music and business. And outside of those
arenas I'm a man of few words. Quiet and shy, really. My wife thinks
I could be a recluse, living the life of the mind with books and beer.
She may be right, but I'd miss her and the girls. I miss them at the
moment, in fact, as I live the life of the mind here in Spain with this
book and some beer. *(Hola, queridas! Yu-hu!)*

What's in a Name?

Then there's the problem of title, which is harder than many think.
You always know what you want to say, but you're rarely sure what to
call what you want to say. This isn't some lame course or training
manual, after all. As of today, there is no title. Here are the ones I've
considered so far, along with the reactions to some of them and who's
doing the reacting:

InterChorus!!

This was the first one I came up with. You know, *"inter"* being Latin
for "among," "between," maybe even "about," but I'm not sure. I still
like it. "Bulls-eye," I thought.

— Allan: "Ah, Bill, no."
— Bill: "But it's catchy, corporate, trendy. Check that capital

in the middle!"
— Allan: "Mmmmm. . . ."
— Bill: "I think the things would fly off the shelves."
— Allan: "It's not dull, that's for sure."
— Bill: "Boy, oh howdy!"
— Allan: "But no."
— Bill: "OK."

— Libby: "Can't do it, Dad."
— Dad: "OK. . . .*Chorus*InterChorus!?"
— Libby: "No, Dad."
— Dad: "OK."

A User's Friendly Guide to the Chorus
or:
A User-Friendly Guide to the Chorus

Emphasis here, see, on the friendly idea: everybody will think that it will be no forbidding task to get through it, choral music for Everyman (P.C. devotees might want to read no further, there's more of the same ahead).

(Dr.) Lisa Graham of Wellesley College rather likes this one, but that could be because she became a (Dr.) at U.S.C. and has taken the courses upon which most of this is based, so she knows what's coming. We both think it's a bit "computer-nerdy," but we also agree that there are a passel of computer nerds in this business, speaking of which,

A Dummy's Guide to the Chorus

was rejected out of hand, as was

BillNotes

Get it? From "Cliff Notes?" Based on my course notes? About music? . . . No, right?

Chorus Confidential

I just like the sound of this one, smacking as it does of James Ellroy's quartet of novels about the L.A. police force, particularly *L.A. Confidential*. Speaking of smacking, I actually stole this from Anthony Bourdain's biographical book — *Kitchen Confidential* — about the chef profession, which I enjoyed reading. Same concept here, really, but with a lot more Here's-What-I-Find-Helpful, and no Naughty Words or references to Naughty Tingly Parts and the uses to which they might be put.

Libby caught the resemblance in purpose and flavor immediately and mentioned it on the phone because she's read Bourdain's book and gave me the sequel for Christmas. And some of the ensuing pages are garnished with culinary similes and metaphors and a smattering of foreign words and what-not.

This title is on my computer desktop folder. It may fly.

Now this:

This is not a work of fiction. Characters, institutions and organizations in this book are, or were, real, and are not used fictitiously. The true names of all innocent persons are used. The names of all guilty persons were changed to protect the innocent from harassment, and the author from lawsuits or rocks through his windows. The author had every intent to describe their actual conduct.

WHO

"What? No CD, No Video?"

Nope. If you want one of those, there are plenty available. Some of them are helpful, some merely self-aggrandizing explorations of limited topics. This book is going to cover a lot of ground about choral music, specifically its nature and its rehearsal. And as any screenwriter knows (often to the dismay of authors, whose only consolation for the adumbrating of their work is a potful of money) it takes much longer to say something on film than it does in a book. As to CDs, we don't learn nearly as much from them about music and its recreation as we do from the primary sources: a live ensemble to listen to; a musical score and an ensemble to rehearse it with; our own inner ears and imaginations.

But don't dismay. If you have read this far, you already have one of the primary qualifications to apply and enjoy what is on these pages. The others are: an interest in the repertoire and medium of the chorus; a basic understanding of musical notation, scales and harmony; rudimentary knowledge of conducting patterns and awareness of the necessity for their clear delivery; the ability to sing a musical line with a fair degree of accuracy once you've learned it – and with a quality that someone besides your mom might admire; an ear which can discern ugly sound and inaccurate pitch; a willingness to learn until you drop. That's it, really. If you are a beginning music student, a choral aficionado, a retired engineer conducting the church choir, a graduate student in choral music, an experienced choral singer who figures she could do a better job than the bozo up front, or an experienced professional who has difficulty wading through the plentiful discussions, workshop sessions and books on techniques and would like to cut to the bare bone, this book is for you.

"Who, Me?"

Because here's the happy, nasty little secret, the confidential part: it's a lot easier to conduct and coach an ensemble - any ensemble - than many would have you believe. So long as you keep two things foremost in your mind: this activity is about only two things, people and music, both of which you must continually serve. It's not about you. (Lord, I wish many of my orchestral colleagues would get that straight. "Maestro," indeed. But more on that later.)

And almost everything on these pages has been said before. If I know (or can remember) where, I'll tell you in the body of the text because I don't want to mess with footnotes, bibliographies and the like. If I don't know where I got it, then it has become my own through teachers, mentors, colleagues, or students, just as what I say to students has become theirs. There is no copyright on what teachers say. If the students want it, they can have it. Some things here are original, however, and I'll be sure to tell you that, too. But as told to us by an ancient Greek, "there is nothing new under the sun." To which I would add that good teaching is a matter of style and *making* "all things new" for yet another generation without falling into the easy traps of cliché, jargon, psycho-babble, trendy buzz-word, or – worst of all – attempts to display to the young how hip we are by "speaking their language."

"Yes, Me"

There's a brief paragraph and a Vita about me at the end of this book. I hope they're impressive because I'm proud of what I've managed to accomplish with luck, Lutheran guilt, a God-given intelligence quotient in three digits, and hard work, in my 60 years of sticking to this planet. I'm also immensely grateful for the profound joy that choral music making has provided and continues to provide. But I did not spring fully mature from the brow of Jove and I am still amazed that my answer to the question above is "yes, by golly, me. I can do this." Your answer can be the same if it isn't already, and to illustrate that I'm going to tell you some things about my background which may encourage you, and which my students have always found surprising when I reveal them in unguarded social moments at retreats or parties. ("Surprising" because of my position and their assumption that, unlike them, I sprang fully mature from the brow of Jove. Many of us are willing to let people believe that, by the way.)

I don't have perfect pitch, I can't play piano, I was not a *wunderkind*, and I'm not a great singer though I'm married to one. As a boy, it was the wife of the basketball coach who taught me to sing in the Methodist Children's Choir (the Lutherans didn't have one). Apparently my voice was pleasing because Billy Dehning achieved a measure of local fame as a boy soprano soloist. My mom bought me a cornet when I was ten (often, over the years, I wished she could have afforded a piano, but such was not the case. Mom did what she could). And I learned to play it from Henry Schultz in the elementary band in the K-12 county school in Aitkin, Minnesota, a town of 1700 (still). I learned pitches and rhythms and a concept of beauty and precision in individual and group sounds from that man. He stopped giving me private lessons when I was 12 because he wanted me to choose between my instrument and baseball. I did. I chose baseball.

Bad decision. I was a slow, inaccurate pitcher with a good curve and a beguiling, wild knuckleball but little else. I stopped playing ball three years later, but kept playing the cornet (graduating in high school to French horn) with agreeable technique and musicality for the next ten years. In high school in California, John Robbins used those instruments to teach me the basic scales, transpositions and rudimentary theory.

So, yes, qualifications for musical leadership should involve knowledge of at least one instrument. For the conductor, piano would be most helpful but barring that, achieving a measure of skill and artistry on any other will do. And yes, singing experience of some kind is also helpful but I didn't sing in a *real* choir until I was 21 years old (when I finally started to formally study music. I didn't formally study voice until I was 24. We Leos are late bloomers).

I played in the band because that was what I knew and because I thought only wusses sang in choirs. (I was wrong again. Gene Simmonds had half the defensive backfield, the quarterback, the star pitcher, and a couple of basketball guards in the mixed choir. Dang, they sounded good, even to an instrumental chauvinist. The wusses sang in the barbershop quartet. Has that changed?)

I started to become a leader when John Robbins said, "Dehning, I'm going to make a drum major out of you." This was when I began to learn the subtle art of command, as well as the conducting patterns of 2, 3 and 4. The latter was easy. It took some time, however, to acquire the ability to stand in front of a group of people and give an order or instruction without sounding like a hopeless wimp on one hand or an arrogant prig on the other. Once I discovered that it was about people and their goals (not just mine) it became easier. Lao Tse said, "If you would lead, follow." Translated, that means give the led what they need to get their job done and then get out of their way; be their teacher, not their master. (I wish some management types could learn this.) I still get nervous, though, when I stand in front of a new group, one that doesn't know or care who or what I am, which happens at least once a year. I sweat like a stallion, and not simply from aerobic exertion; it's nerves and insecurity, sweetheart, and I just turned sixty (have I said that?). But I figure if I ever lose that doubt, that insecurity, I will be the lesser for it and so will those around me. We will not accomplish, much less enjoy.

With the foregoing minimal qualifications, I stepped in front of my first chorus when I was nineteen and have been in front of at least two every year since. And boy, have I improved!

"Yes, You"

The final qualifications for choral leadership are ones at which we must work until we relinquish that leadership or until we die, whichever occurs first:

- A continual effort to become a clearer, more expressive visual conductor.
- A continual interest in how the voice works, both individually and in ensemble.
- A continual broad interest in history, philosophy, literature and poetry.
- And a continuing, inviolable interest in humankind's finest achievement – language, starting with our native one.

We do not have to have all these things before we step in front of our first ensemble. God forbid. I didn't study German until I was 40, for example, and it is now my second language. When I finish with this for the day, I'm going to work on my Spanish for an hour, something that I haven't done for 45 years. So there's hope for you, too, regardless of where you are on the continuum from desire to artistry. We learn what we must when we must – you will dive into orchestration before you step in front of that first orchestra. But we learn only if we're interested:

> Interest is the key to life,
> Interest in the clue.
> Interest is the drum and fife,
> And any god will do.
> – The Keener's Manual

Not interest in the "answer," mind you, but in the "clue." If you're looking for answers here you've come to the wrong place. I can only give you some choices, some clues and a few of the right questions. Thus everything in the subsequent chapters is intentionally pithy, is *essence* – the pure, distilled ingredients of a perfume present in one vessel – me. The oils and alcohol necessary for you to dilute this *essence* – to fabricate, enrich and distribute your own *eau de toilette* – are available in dozens of books and articles on the various subjects represented here, as well as within that most necessary and unique of sources, Your Own Precious Self.

THE SCORE

Interpretation is the ability to make musical ideas clear.   – C.P.E. Bach
Interpretation is the beautifully simple result of total understanding.
               – Ingolf Dahl

We Americans have an enduring fascination with technique. We are the "can-do" folks and are justifiably proud of that. Many cultures around the world try to emulate us in this regard. But reflection and *savoir-faire* are not our strong suits, just as history for us tends not to extend past last Tuesday. We are more interested in the sense than in the sound of language, for instance. But style is all. If a choice arises between form and content, I'll choose form every time (and so will my daughters, because I drilled it into them). Don't get me wrong here, both are necessary. Form without content is the mark of the dilettante, just as content without form is the mark of the pedant. But technique is acquired in order to get something done. In music, technique is acquired in order to *render a convincing interpretation of the score*. Period. Next question, please. I'll put this quite boldly: **interpretation is the most important thing that we do.** To borrow from St. Paul: for conductors, these three abide – interpretation, conducting and rehearsing, but the greatest of these is interpretation.

And just to establish my *bona fides* once again, I am told by long-time students and respected contemporary colleagues that they are my three strengths, though some might disagree about the order of the latter two. No one has ever accused a chorus under my direction of being perfectly in tune like the Scandinavians or perfectly together like the Prussians (though we work very hard at both). But they are always described as musical, which means something hit home; someone sighed with longing or hooted with delight at the appropriate times and not only in spirituals. After a recent competition in Europe with the U.S.C. Chamber Choir (which we won, so the intonation and precision couldn't have been *too* bad), Judge Maria Guinand (whom I respect far more than is necessary or desirable to relate here) came up to me and said, "They sing from the heart, Mr. Dehning, and that is the most important thing." And *my* young heart sang all the way back to the funky hotel.

Indeed, I am weary unto numbness of hearing perfect renderings of musical notation with perfect choral technique – and often "balletically" conducted – which say nothing at all to the human spirit because no human imagination has been involved in the score's realization but only Spartan drill in the rehearsal and a fulsome measure of personal vanity in the conducting. We not only hear and think, people, we *feel*, too. Yin and yang and yong (I made that last one up) are inseparable. And yes, as Bruno Walter said, "There is no substitute for correctness." We've got to get it right but we have to do so in order that what the performer expresses, and what the listener perceives, are convincing (notice I didn't say "right"). And conviction is found at the intersection of study, thought and risk. Risk. Look if you like, but you have to leap. You must choose. Even to *not* choose is to choose, friends. And it ain't what you say, it's the way what you say it.

Choices

At the young Oregon Bach Festival back in 1975, Steve Fuller and I managed to ask Helmuth Rilling out for dinner so as to pick his brain and discover the Secret to his edifying rehearsals and thrilling interpretations, especially the latter. So just before the steaks, I ventured the question that would reveal the simple Truth: "How does one study a score?" His puzzled response? "You look at it." (See? I told you all this was easier than many imagine.) Boy, were we struck dumb! For a more detailed emanation from the Bach Festival, take a look at Tom Somerville's excellent handout to festival conducting participants regarding score analysis in the Appendix (page 151). Good as it is, though, and no matter what else you may learn from some of the fine essays on the topic found elsewhere, interpretation of a score starts with those four words above.

Another anecdote: as a graduate student at USC in 1968, I was asked to conduct the Concert Choir during James Vail's sabbatical leave. We were involved with the orchestra that semester and Ingolf Dahl was conducting the combined performance. One of the pieces he chose was Webern's *Das Augenlicht*. I was 25, had never done a 12-tone piece in my life and was scared poopless. I asked for a meeting to go over the score with him and I arrived armed with graph paper, rulers, slide rules (this was before calculators), Vernier calipers, and other technical accouterments with which to attempt to discern the 12-tone rows and figure out how to teach the dang thing. The meeting lasted five minutes.

— "Put all that away, Mr. Dehning, go to a piano and play it over and
   over until you hear it."
— "But Mr. Dahl," I replied (don't you just love that Olde Worlde
   formality? I do; I miss it except when I'm in Europe, to which I
   repair as often as financially possible), "I can't play the piano."
— "Then it will just take you longer, Mr. Dehning. Play one line at a
   time and one "chord" at a time until you hear it in your head and
   can respond to the chorus if they sing it wrong."

I blessed Jehovah that the piece was only five minutes long and must
tell you, after that experience, analyzing scores in common practice
became quite easy and learning anthems for my church choir became
a lead pipe cinch. That's because my inner ear improved. I developed
a concept of the piece and I had the consequent conviction to rehearse
it. This happened because I was forced to take a risk and wrestle with
the difficult. But that was merely wrestling; in order to lose our fear of
the difficult we must not only confront it, we must become fascinated
by it – almost infatuated with it. Once that happens, we realize that the
difficult is understandable and has a solution, too, and that we were not
afraid of the difficult *per se*, but afraid of what humans have always
been afraid of – the unknown. And the only unknown that cannot
become knowable is death. The rest are easy by comparison.

Notice in both anecdotes above that neither teacher suggested I go find
a recording and learn it that way. And this is our **first choice** in
interpretation: how to learn the score. The answer is Rilling's and
Dahl's: you look at it and if you can't hear it by looking at it, you play
elements of it at a keyboard until you can; you get your clues from the
raw material – the score – not someone else's recreation of it. My
further answer is: then we take it into rehearsal and work on it until it's
almost in the ensemble. THEN we go listen to a recording and/or play
it for them to get other ideas and approaches.

"What? No CD, No Video?"

Nope. And not because of the usual response to this question, which
is that you would be influenced by someone else's interpretation.

There's nothing whatever wrong with being influenced by Gardiner or Ericsson or Shaw or Herreweghe. I think they've got some pretty good ideas, don't you? No, the problem with learning a score from a recording is that we learn it from the outside in, not from the inside out. The latter helps the score to become an integral part of YOU. It enables you to develop two of the most important "C" words in your work: Concept and Conviction (the third is Courtesy, but that's for another chapter). Without those two C-words we cannot begin to rehearse and we cannot begin to conduct because we have nothing to say, and who needs yet another conductor with nothing to say? *The ability to say, "here's why" is important.* The second choice we make is to ascertain the primary aesthetic – or spirit – from which the work springs. We do this by examining the parameters of vocal music (text, melody, harmony, rhythm, form, sonority, texture, and dynamic) and deciding whether the evidence reveals it to be a "circle" or a "square." Which geometrical shape it is will guide all subsequent decisions and choices we make regarding the work, and is the overriding factor in our Concept of the work. I got this stylistic geometry idea from Charles Hirt thirty-six years ago. To make it clear, we need to set up some synonyms and antonyms from human psychology, philosophy and history.

CIRCLE	**SQUARE**
Emotional	Rational
Intuitive	Deductive
Organic	Formal
Yin	Yang
Asymmetrical	Symmetrical
Romantic	Classic
Abandon	Restraint
Dionysian	Apollonian
Roman	Hellenic
Libertarian	Republican
Anarchism	Authoritarianism
"Whoopee!"	"Easy, big fella..."
Flexible	*Rigid.*
	Conservative

Enough? Getting the idea? Well, we can do the same thing with periods of music, art, or political history:

CIRCLE	SQUARE
Gothic	Renaissance
Baroque	Classical
Romantic	Impressionist
12-tone	Neo-Classic
Neo-Romanticism	???

I'm going to use only one or two musical parameters in several periods as examples to illustrate how this works. You get to do the rest.

Rhythm in gothic music is complex, often disjunct, and tends to lope along with abandon. The **text** in sacred renaissance music is directed toward God, not man, thus melody is restrained in range and tends to be simple and step-wise. **Melodies** in baroque music tend to be highly melismatic, ornamented and "spun" out in an organic, rather than derived fashion; **texture** tends to be dense. **Form** in classical music is derived from beautifully symmetrical phrases and is compact, textures are clean, and harmonic rhythm is stately compared to the baroque. **Dynamic** in romantic music is exploited for its own sake (two *ff*s are no longer enough, nor are two *pp*s); **harmony** is sensual; forms lengthen considerably – a Bach passion takes three hours, a Mozart symphony forty minutes, a Wagner opera can take five days (or does it just seem that way?); emotional and sonic excess become a way of life.

The aesthetic decision for me in these common practice historical periods is which of the parameters I'm going to make certain come through to the singer and the audience. And I must be aware that there is really no such thing as the perfect circle or the perfect square; art and people are more complex than that. Brahms has a very big square within his circle (form and fugue – in fact, it's possible that Brahms was the *only* romantic figure who could write a real fugue). As a result, I try to make certain that musical subjects are evident and I refrain from dynamic excess in his music. And part of the reason I enjoy Vittoria a bit more than Palestrina is that he has a big circle within his square (more piquant dissonances), thus I feel I can be a bit more dramatic with dynamic and tempo alteration (the same may be true of Haydn or Mozart – Haydn has more daring harmonic "purple patches" than Mozart). And so on.

"Fine," you say, "but what about contemporary and twentieth century pieces which are not part of the foregoing historical periods? What then?" To begin with, I'll tell you right now that the majority of the published works are neo-romantic. This is because the lush harmonies and singable melodies are what we know because it's what we hear most of the time. Look at most symphony and opera programs; look at most church choir and high school repertoire (not, paradoxically, most fine children's choir programs, thanks to people like Anne Tomlinson). And it's not because all of the music is technically easy. Much of it is not; a Mozart or Lassus canon is far easier. No, it's what we, our singers and audiences know and respond to. I'm told that one highly successful televangelist's wife will not even allow a piece in a minor key to be performed in the service. Probably not "upbeat" enough. (Do yourself a favor, go find the hymn tune *Ebenezer* and tell me it isn't a great, uplifting tune, minor mode or not. Put it with a great text and you've got yourself some artistic and emotional dynamite.)

As a result of this preponderance of "circular" contemporary music, the spirit of most of the really fine "square" pieces out there is consistently violated – nay, slain outright. I'll use two overwhelmingly popular examples, Duruflé's *Ubi Caritas* and Lauridsen's *Dirait-on* . I'll also use the Lauridsen piece to demonstrate the decisions to be made once we've determined the aesthetic of a piece.

We don't have to KNOW that *Ubi Caritas* quotes Gregorian chant almost exactly (remember I said you could make these decisions using the score alone?), we could certainly figure out that it is chantlike, though, by playing or singing the melody a few times. It has that modal, ethereal, flow to it, plus it has that non-metrical feel, a feeling which almost becomes fact and hits us upside the head when we notice with a cursory glance that the meter changes almost every other bar. And we can further confirm that the melody is the dominant parameter in the piece when we note that the harmony moves with the melody in textual phrases and not note by note. The harmonic rhythm is quite slow, in other words. This latter clue, plus the clue that the harmonies are subtly flavored with those typically French non-chord tones are what seduce the unsuspecting (or non-discerning) into slowing the tempo of this little piece down to an indulgent ooze. And never mind what the composer indicated for the tempo of the quarter note, which I think I remember is around 66. I've heard performances where the *eighth* note was 80. And squirmed all the way through them. Of course, to most listeners it's lovely because those are luscious harmonies that would make even your mother-in-law twitch in her seat. But it's not what Duruflé wrote. The *spirit* is all wrong, thus all other decisions (tempo, too much *rubato*, excessive lingering on certain chords) make this gentle whiff of Chanel® a hormone-drenched blast of Brut®. It turns simple devotion into complicated lust and turns something French into something German (I've nothing against either lust or Germans. I do have something against Brut®).

A similar overindulgence in sensuality afflicts Lauridsen's *Dirait-on* (quite possibly the most performed piece in the repertoire since its publication), an inability to simply let it be – or let it be simple. According to the composer, this is a simple cabaret song and, as usual with Lauridsen or any other fine composer who understands poetry, he has indicated quite clearly what he wants in terms of dynamic, tempo and rubato. It's not as though it were an older piece of music in which a good deal of sleuthing is often required to determine the basic decisions conductors must make in such cases for lack of clues from the composer himself. Here, then, are those basic decisions: fast/slow; loud/soft, breath/phrase, long/short.

Tempo

Decisions regarding tempo hinge on the factors of tempo indication, if any (*Andante*? *Vivace*?), textual mood and delivery (devout? ebullient? melismatic? syllabic?), rhythmic clarity (halves? quarters? sixteenths?), texture (homophonic? polyphonic?), harmonic rhythm (fast? slow?). The latter is often forgotten and is most exemplified in Bach chorales. In these pieces the harmonic rhythm (the rate at which the harmony changes) is usually on every pulse (quarter note) and occasionally every half pulse. That is one reason (historical considerations aside) that this music is done at a rather stately tempo

– the harmonies need time to unfold. To go too fast would blur them, especially in a live acoustic. Most Bach chorales are not performed at a frisky clip.

When examining a piece for tempo, I look at all of the foregoing factors, sing some melodies and rhythms and start to tap out a pulse and take it into rehearsal. Then and only then (you heard it here) do I look at the metronome marking (if any) and see how close I am. I suppose because of my early training as a drum major, I'm usually spot-on or one or two clicks away (I'll never forget mm = 120). If I'm not close, I always try the composer's metronome marking first. If she's a fine composer, she's usually right and I will accede to her wishes. If he's questionable, or if I honestly feel I can represent the *spirit* of the piece better with my tempo (say, because I have a small group in a dry acoustic), I'll use mine.

But let's give these folks the benefit of the doubt and try to move at least in the same zip code as their tempo. For *Dirait-on*, Lauridsen wants 104; many people want to make more of the melody than is there and move at 80. This slows down not only the melody, but turns the relatively slow harmonic rhythm into a bagpipe drone. As to tempo alteration, *poco* is Italian for "a little," and this piece is a square, so don't overdo the rubato; let it roll unless the score asks for a "little" *ritard* (there's only one "molto" and it's – yup – near the end). And *ritards* are used to delineate form, which is why most pieces or movements end with a *ritard* – it lets Uncle Fred know that the form is over. The only other reason to add one that is not marked would be to highlight a surprising or particularly colorful cadence, or a dramatic word (very dramatic). Otherwise, exercise restraint with the use of tempo alteration, whether the piece is a circle or a square, but especially if it's a square. Let it be.

As to pre-Beethoven music with only Italian indications of mood and approximate tempo, I'll relate another anecdote from the Rilling seminars of long ago. I am not the interrogator:
— "Mr. Rilling, in Bach's music, exactly what is meant by Andante?"
— "Not fast."
— "And Allegro?"
— "Not slow."

There you go. . .

Dynamic

I'll have a lot more to say about dynamic in the chapters on the Ensemble. For now it's enough to say that unless the composer specifically indicates it, dynamic decisions depend on many of the same factors which affect those of tempo. It's vocally difficult to perform a melismatic line at *forte*, for example, so I take a bit off of the dynamic; it's difficult to hear the subject in a fugue if all other parts are too loud, so I give the subject a chance by reducing dynamic in other parts (and the "head" of the subject is more important than the "tail" because the initial point of imitation is what the audience hears).

Speaking of balance, in an older score – say, one by Bach – when full winds are playing, including trumpets, it's a good idea to mark the chorus *forte* whether Bach has or not. This is a decision which takes texture into consideration and the converse is also true: if only the continuo is playing, or strings alone, we could reduce the chorus to *mf* or less, or reduce the chorus to a semi-chorus. In fact, in many major works from the eighteenth and nineteenth centuries, I spend a lot of time in study trying to determine where the poor chorus doesn't have to sing *forte*; where they can do something besides continue to bellow.

Speaking of bellowing, one of the other keys to dynamic is to be aware of the High-Fast-Loud/Low-Slow-Soft Syndrome, toward which all ensembles have a propensity (you heard it here; Charles Hirt was impressed when I first came up with this in 1966). As becomes evident with some thought, this syndrome also affects tempo and tessitura, but we're talking dynamic at the moment. It isn't required, for example, that a high, fast musical event be loud. It just wants to be and ensembles tend to perform it that way. All we have to do is be aware of this tendency and alert to what our ensemble is doing.

In specific regard to the Lauridsen piece, it's the *fortes* which tend to be out of bounds, especially in the imitative section which needs emphasis on only the first few notes to make the imitation clear. The text and melody alone, however, would indicate a subdued dynamic throughout, even if Lauridsen had submitted no clues in this regard. In fact, I'll occasionally test our choral conducting students in interpretation. I'll take a piece of music they probably haven't heard, Wite Out® the composer's dynamic marks, photocopy it, distribute it, and ask that they look at all musical parameters and derive the dynamics from them. Here's the point: in a well-written piece, the dynamics become self-evident. A good composer doesn't write a piece and then consult the *I Ching* to determine dynamic. It is as much a part of the fabric as melody and rhythm.

Breath/Phrase

This is the first decision I make, even before ones of tempo and dynamic, and I'm not sure why. Possibly it's because my analytical process begins with form, not so I can put a name to it but so I have a rough idea of what's going on. Then the rough idea becomes smoother as form becomes clearer and I am able to make the subsequent interpretive decisions more easily. Maybe I'm just a formal kind of guy: shape – the big picture – is important to me.

Then, too, a chorus operates on breath, and the end of a phrase is usually where a breath is taken, but not always (see below). And the sooner the chorus coordinates breath, the sooner it will sing with freedom, so I want to inculcate breath early in the rehearsal process. Also, breathing is a rhythmic process. But more on breath and rhythm in rehearsal later.

Some occasions to NOT breathe at the end of a phrase:
- Before a large, upward leap in the melodic voice, usually the soprano – I want the voices to take such intervals "on the breath" lest they stab, lunge at, blurt, blast (well, you get the idea) the upper note.
- After the second eighth note with quarter pulse (even if in only one voice), especially at a brisk tempo. There simply isn't time to get this done smoothly and/or together, and the rewards are not worth the rehearsal time necessary to achieve it. Better to avoid it; take the easy way out. I advise students to take the easy way out whenever possible. (This is not sin or sloth. The entire profession and craft of engineering is based on taking the easiest possible way out. Why should we be different? Because "easy" is associated with loose morals? Nonsense. And no, there is still no easy way to learn a score. If there were, I would write it here and the entire choral profession would pay me homage.)

- If the ends of textual and musical phrase do not coincide, we might choose to favor text and not breathe. (This is one of the ways to improve hymn-singing with your church congregation, by the way, though I hope you have better luck than I did.)

The final decision to make regarding breath is where the *time* to breathe is going to come from. We have two choices: 1) we can cheat the value of the note before the breath, in which case the pulse is uninterrupted; 2) we can give the notes on either side of the breath full value, in which case the pulse is interrupted in order to breathe. Choice One prevails the majority of the time, especially if the tempo is breezy. Choice Two is often a very musical, expressive one to make, but the tempo must be relaxed. Also, over-use of Choice Two – constantly interrupting the pulse with the consequent, constant choral lurch for breath which can result – has been known to provoke sea-sickness in the most dauntless of listeners. It's much like tarragon in cooking.

Articulation

In the Pantheon of Conductorial Decisions, this god is least worshiped among choral conductors, many of whom stand as infidels before her altar unaware of what she can do for them. Everybody understands the need for loud/soft, fast/slow and most understand the need for phrase definition and breath. Few, in my experience, are truly cognizant of the raw artistic *possibilities* that short/long has to offer. Thar's gold in them thar hills, amigos. Samuel Morse made a whole new code out of dots and dashes. Imagine what they can do for us!

Instrumentalists understand dots and dashes and slurs more readily because they learn them earlier. I could play exact notes, rhythms and dynamics on my cornet for Henry Schultz but he wouldn't let me go unless the dots and dashes were right, too. It was the only way to get out of there and onto the pitcher's mound. But of course, I forgot all this in my first experience with chorus and orchestra (yeah, it was the Vivaldi *Gloria*). When the concert mistress asked me how I wanted the first few bars to go, I gave her a puzzled look and said...

— "Well, you know, bum-BUM-bum-bum-bum-BUM-bum-bum-bum."

— "Long or short? How do you want it bowed?"

I will tell you, at that moment ignorance was not bliss. I dusted off my orchestration book that night, did a crash course on bowing that I should have passed several years ago, and learned that string bowing pretty much determines articulation. (See? We learn what we must *when* we must. Better late than never, in this case.) As a former brass player I was ready with suggestions as to slurring or tonguing, but I had just come off an eight-hour swing shift at Bethlehem Steel before my 9:00 a.m. string techniques class and was less than alert (no excuse, of course).

With voices it's different, though. For one thing, the voice is the most naturally *legato* instrument in God's firmament. There's a reason many instrumental parts are marked *cantabile*, and that so many instrumental conductors yell, "SING, damn you!" Except for good string players, *legato* is not inherent in instrumental technique, they have to work at it. Pianists will kill for it. For singers, on the other hand, *short* notes are the problem, because short, or *staccato* notes, are not natural to vocal technique. The vowel needs time to speak.

Staccato doesn't really mean "short," you know, it means "separate." It means that there is a moment of silence between the notes. How long that silence is depends entirely on interpretation or concept. Singers trying to sing "*staccato*" usually sing too "short" and can (mostly *do*) sound unmusical or, worse, accented. I prefer the word "detached," which psychologically tends to shorten the silence the singers perform, OR I tell them to go immediately to the consonant, which is the most musical and vocal way to sing detached (you heard it here). By heading directly to the consonant, the time to perceive the vowel (which carries 99% of the sound) is reduced and the note *sounds* separate, even though the singer hasn't physically "separated" anything at all.

Much of deciding to "head for the consonant" depends on how the words *want* to come out of the mouth in the rhythm in which they are notated. "Put the text in your mouth," I tell our students, "listen to what happens, or doesn't happen. What *wants* to happen?" ("Want to" is a whole 'nother topic and has many levels. "Want to" may be the most important two words in this book. More later? You bet.) I'll give two examples of how this can work.

The Sanctus of Rheinberger's *Cantus Missae* lines out the words *Benedictus qui venit* in equal quarters after a quarter rest. This could well be performed *legato*: – – – – – – – , but it wants to come out: – – ~ ~ – – – because of the tendency to head for the consonant on the syllables *"dic-tus."* This approach gives a real delicacy to the line it wouldn't have performing it *legato*. After rehearsing it this way for some time, alto Kuan-Fen Liu asked after rehearsal why I had made that choice (Boy, I love such questions, especially after rehearsal, not during). I told her that it was not at all necessary or required, that it just made the line more *interesting* in my opinion (there's that word again).

A similar situation occurs in the compound duple portion at the end of Bach's *Komm, Jesu, Komm*, which moves in eighths (capitals are two eighths): *Die WAHRheit UND das LE- - - - - - -* (long melisma) *-ben*. *"Das"* wants to come out short, so we let it (the easy way out, yes?). I didn't have to say a word. Also, the bass line on the long melisma of *"Leben"* lopes along in series of three eighths which I was simply allowing the basses to sing all *legato* because I hadn't thought of it otherwise – it was a simple bass continuo function for the upper voices, so I ignored it.

At our peril: the basses were consistently behind tempo and were performing as basses often do – as though hungover. I finally got frustrated after frequent remonstrations to be more precise, and during a break asked the section leader, Bob Duff, what he thought the problem was, because the basses weren't – *mirabile dictu* – stupid. He said he thought it was the articulation. So I "bowed" the whole melisma for them at the next break. Instead of performing the notes all long, I marked *most* of them as long-long-short / long-long-short, with the occasional three longs.

It worked. The basses were no longer behind tempo, much to the whinnying delight of the sopranos in front of them. Moreover, the line now had a lilt and a forward movement that had never been there before, all because of that single short note (or "up-bow"). The previously soggy bassline was now *al dente*. In other words, the line was now more musical, not because of dynamic or phrase or tempo but because of articulation.

The short-and-long of it is the spice added to the other ingredients in the stew, and spices must be added to the dish during the cooking process, not afterward. You can adjust them, as we did at Bob Duff's suggestion above, but they really should be there from the beginning. Careful thought and experimentation with articulation as it relates to text and texture is one of the master keys to the kingdom of my vaunted musicality. Bob's too. But enough metaphor, it's time to finish this up.

Now that we have studied and hummed and thought and experimented with all parameters of the piece and their possible execution, now that we've *looked at* the score and played it for hours, we will have formed our *Concept* of it (not the only one, not the "right" one) and acquired the degree of *Conviction* (not rectitude) necessary to convince (not brainwash) our ensemble that we have an idea of what we think the *Composer* may have intended. Note that last clause (long as it is). It's the composer and the music that we and the ensemble are trying to serve, not the reputation of the church or school, the group's collective ego, or (whoo boy!) our reputations and egos. *It's about the music*, whether the music is *Komm, Jesu, Komm*, or *Come Fly With Me*. (That last clause in italics – *It's about the music* – is something else even my enemies say about me and my work, by the way. It's also maybe the reason I'm neither rich nor famous (not the enemies, the italic clause. Well, *maybe* the enemies. Both of them.)

THE CRAFT

Someone besides me is going to have to do it, but we need to make a name change from ACDA to ACCA, from American Choral "Directors" to American Choral "Conductors." More important, we're all going to have to do this for ourselves in our heads. Why? Because once the music has been ordered, studied and rehearsed; once the principal/minister/dean/headmaster has been mollified; once the tour money has been raised and the bills paid and the parents/booster clubs/committees/bursars are all happy; once all the social conflicts in the ensemble have been resolved and all the individual counseling has been done and the room is clean; conducting is what we *do*. "Conductor" is what we *are*. In performance we have to finally shut up. As soon as we step in front of that ensemble in rehearsal and begin to lift the right hand, we are interpreting with gesture, whether we think we are or not. There is no choice here. Technique is the means, interpretation is the end.

Other Ways of Doing It

I know. You and I both know people who don't have excellent stick technique and their groups sound fantastic every time we hear them. They are either Golden Tongues or Pied Pipers. Golden Tongues (GTs) get it done in rehearsal with persuasive words, eloquent words, colorful words. GTs have tremendously pictorial vocabularies and are frequently very intelligent, well-traveled people with charismatic personalities. Howard Swan and Charles Hirt were two such people, as is Paul Salamunovich (but he has good stick technique, too). Swan's visual technique was often clumsy; Hirt's often unintelligible, but boy did their groups sing, even the honor groups with which they had spent little time. They were magical men. Another one who didn't have the most striking visual technique was Robert Shaw. But his obsessions and his incandescent intelligence more than carried the day for him. As we look over the cases above, I wouldn't recommend that any of us try this at home.

Pied Pipers (PPs) are rousingly good recruiters and smooth politicians (in the good sense). PPs get it done *before* the rehearsing even starts.

They have gathered the political, financial and diplomatic resources to form a posse, head out to the range, rope some prize cattle and bring them back to the corral. They have fine choruses because they have good *singers*. Also, as the metaphor Pied Piper suggests, they have very charismatic personalities. William Hall is a Pied Piper (and a very evocative conductor).

How can we determine at an early stage in our careers which we are? What can we do to become better Golden Tongues and Pied Pipers? We don't. We can't – very little beyond reading outside of our field in the first case and smiling in a roomful of strangers in the second. What we can do is work diligently our entire careers to become better conductors. Because I'll tell you this: even if we have the most golden of tongues in rehearsal, even if we have the political acumen of Machiavelli's Prince, we will still get it done more quickly, efficiently and enjoyably for all if we are fine conductors. One gesture is worth a thousand words. And here's another instance of our confidential, nasty little secret: it's easier than many would have us believe. We need more autobiography here.

My Story Again

I became a conductor because I had no choice (not the best of reasons but better than none, wouldn't you say?). When I finally decided to study music at 21, I had to decide what it was I might be good at. I knew I wasn't going to be a world-beater as a trumpet player and I hadn't taken a single voice lesson (my gorgeous boy soprano voice had become something quite other). Conducting looked easier than either of the foregoing so I decided I might as well study that. Besides, I had been a fair athlete and thus had a fair amount of physical coordination. It seemed to be as good a choice as any.

I was right, it was easier, though I had to battle demons my entire life that abide with me to this day: lack of keyboard skill and lack of perfect pitch. The lack of keyboard skill meant I couldn't follow the usual orchestral conducting path, which was to go to an opera house in Europe, bang out parts for the singers and the chorus, be allowed to conduct the matinees that nobody else wanted, eventually graduating to some of the evening performances and migrating back home to the U.S., feigning a "Euro" accent, charming the women on the Board, and finally hopping up on some podium somewhere. (This path is still being used today, along with another one: rich people simply buying choruses and orchestras. Some of these people are very good. Some are wretched. But good singers and players can perform with anybody, they just "do the dots" if what is moving in front of them lacks craft or art.)

Since that avenue was blocked, I figured I could at least keep my demons at bay with good, old-fashioned, northwoods Minnesota hard work, lots of it, and become a choral conductor. As it turned out, I have studied or taught conducting technique my entire career (we always learn more than we teach) and it worked: I'm a good conductor. Here's what I learned and what I taught.

The Basics

I am not one of those (and there are many, though they all protest innocence) who insists that students in our conducting classes and lessons conduct like their teacher. I have children; I don't need Dehning clones. And like my children, I want our students to be independent human beings with their unique expressive capabilities. What are they expressing?

Their concept of the score. That is the first basic. And the degree of conviction they have about their concept of the score will be revealed in their gesture. The craft of conducting is one of gesture and/or mime, and conviction is a three-dollar word for "want to." On countless occasions when the student is having difficulty showing something with gesture – especially when I am asked to demonstrate how I might conduct the example – I ask them how they want it to go. They explain in words; I assent and reply, "Then want it more and try again."

This is not a facile response, but is based on another fundamental principle I learned from Charles Hirt and never forgot: *the body tends to coordinate when it knows what it wants to say.* Athletes know this: *see* the ball going over the plate; *see* the ball going over the front of the rim; don't look at the spot you want to hit the tennis ball, watch the ball and *see* it going to the spot. Keep your eye on the ball (for us, the "ball" is the score – or more accurately, our interpretation of it). We have to want it. And want it again and again. We may not get what we want – we often don't – but we will never get it if we don't want it. Great things can happen when we "keep our eye on the ball" while conducting. (As we shall see later, the same is true in rehearsal.)

And we must continue to look at our own work through the magic of videotape. Put a camera on a performance from the back and on a rehearsal from the front from time to time. See what you like and what annoys you. Rejoice in what you like. Work on what annoys you. Remember that our effort here is to continually become better: clearer and more evocative as conductors (so that we can become ACCA). No one should be above this self-criticism, but don't be like me and beat yourself up about it.

Don't practice gestures with recordings, either – the ensemble will respond whether you want it to or not. Practice gestures as you go through the score in your head ("now how am I going to show this?")

I haven't practiced gesture with a recording since my very first conducting class (nor have I ever taught a class with recordings). I could never get George Szell to take my tempo or hold fermatas the same length as I. Funny how that works. Let's leave recordings to our orchestral brothers and sisters – that's how many of them commit scores to memory. Real conductors commit scores to memory with time, hard work or gifts. I don't have a photographic memory but by the time I've rehearsed and performed the work once, it has become memorized through process. Which is why the second time through a score is so much fun: I can *rehearse* it from memory, thereby hearing far better. The problem here, of course, is that our repertoire – unlike standard instrumental repertoire – is so vast that in our zeal to experience as much of it as possible for our own growth we often don't get to perform pieces twice, much less thrice or more. The only piece, for instance, I have done more than three times is Bach's *Singet dem Herrn ein neues Lied*. I could perform that piece straight on into eternity. I just may.

Patterns

Robert Frost said that "there may be more poetry outside of verse, more education outside of school, more love outside of marriage. In fact, there may be more of anything outside of any institution than there is in it. But I'm kind of an institutional man, really."

So am I. There may be more music outside of a pattern than within it (and many conductors – not just choral conductors – seem determined to explore all that music) but I believe in patterns. I have never had orchestral players get lost or confused with me in front of them; they know where I am on every pulse (and not because I give every cue, I don't. But more on that later). And yes, I could wander all over the place when a piece is in four for 573 bars but I usually don't, even with a chorus, which can see the whole score and deduce where I am. Nossir, I stick to the rules 99% of the time and you should too. So learn the patterns and use them, you hear?

Some Definitions

We can find these patterns almost anywhere, but I still recommend Elizabeth Green's *The Modern Conductor*, which is lucid and succinct. Much of what I have to say in the ensuing pages starts with what she has to say on a lot of topics. I will alter and add to many things she has said, but the general ideas are often the same. (Go see for yourself and compare.) I also learned an immense amount watching James Vail teach beginning conducting at USC, and Helmuth Rilling teach advanced conducting at the Oregon Bach Festival. They have been models for me every time I teach this particular topic.

A pattern consists of a number of beats. A beat – or Beat – for our purposes here has three parts in its anatomy: ictus, rebound and direction. (Pay attention here, because I'm going to be referring to this anatomy a lot.) Each anatomical part of the Beat gives the ensemble specific information.

The direction of the Beat tells them *which* pattern we are conducting and where we are in that pattern. The ictus tells them exactly *when* the pulse of the Beat occurs; it is the lowest and fastest part of the Beat. The rebound tells them everything else about the Beat, most specifically *how* the next Beat is to be performed. A preparatory gesture is simply the rebound of the beat before, with some additions.

Physically, the rebound is a muscular reflex action which occurs in accordance with a fundamental principle of physics: every action has an equal and opposite reaction. The harder you push a basketball down, the higher it will bounce. The harder you strike the ictus of the Beat, the higher the rebound will (should) bounce. Rebound is the spring or "boing" in the pattern, partly because all beats are, essentially, "downbeats," and what goes down often wants to come back up – in this case because of muscular reflex action.

So, these three abide: ictus, direction and rebound, but the greatest of these is rebound because it is the How of the Beat; it embodies that holiest of holies – style. Direction and ictus give us Content; rebound gives us Form.

Moves

Every craft requires a set of tools and conducting is no exception. In order not to lose those tools we need a box to keep them in. My term for the tool box is the **Home Base** pattern: it is *mf*, non-*legato*, andante; it displays clearly, but by no means emphatically, all aspects of the Beat – ictus, rebound, direction. It is dull, actually, because it is comfortable for us and we are not trying to make any statement – fashion, musical or otherwise. Not yet. It is us in our slippers reading the paper on Saturday morning.

"Comfortable" for most conductors means the stand is no higher than the navel and not too close, so that the head doesn't look straight down, obscuring the first and most important tool, the eyes. "Comfortable" for most conductors can be defined as loose yet ready posture (like a good, well-trained singer, proud pectorals and all), with the pattern in the high strike zone (from beneath the neck to above the pierced navel), and with the forearm generally parallel to the floor and elbows comfortably away from the sides, not pinned to them and not lifted up to the shoulders in the Angry Chicken pose.

This latter concept is called "plane of activity" and it can vary. We can move above this general plane for lighter/softer sound, and we can move a bit below it for heavier/more powerful sound. But don't get stuck at either extreme. Most conductors conduct too high (often because the stand is too high); a few get stuck at the beltline.

Now let's put some tools in that box. The following tools are all that is necessary to be a clear conductor but we must be a master – not an apprentice – of all of them. And make no mistake, for the conductor, Clarity is next to Godlity (you heard it here).

Hammer and Saw

First of all, a **preparatory gesture** does not include an obnoxiously audible nasal snort (Lord, that's annoying). A preparatory gesture is the rebound of the beat before, but it does not include its ictus. This movement is always upward, and it has more height and energy than normal because it must catch the eye and because of the physical principle of inertia: a body at rest wants to stay there (it takes more energy to start a car rolling than it does to keep it rolling, hence using more fuel).

The upward movement says READY and is the preparatory command; delivery of the ensuing ictus says GO and is the command of execution. The preparatory command is by far the more important. Sometimes in rehearsal I give a monster preparatory command and then turn and walk away. The ensemble comes in anyway (fun, huh?). A preparatory gesture occurs not only at the beginning of a piece or movement but throughout the music, because it is also used to prepare moves other than the initial preparatory: the ones which follow.

The **release** – or "cut-off" as some so brutally put it – is the same as that of the preparatory, except that its function is reversed: instead of beginning a musical event, it is used to end it. And again it takes a bit more energy because of inertia: a moving body wants to stay moving. It begins with the higher rebound of the beat before and can then finish with the standard loop down and to the right. This loop is universally recognized and is the most emphatic method; if in doubt or in front of a festival choir of 600, I use it.

Often though, the release can be accomplished by simply delivering the next ictus, if it occurs on a rest. At the end of a piece or movement, we can accomplish the release by giving an imaginary downbeat after the double bar. This is the most subtle method and the one I use the most.

A **fermata** involves use of both of the previous moves and is not a move in itself. It goes like this: higher rebound on the beat before the fermata – preparatory command (pc); delivery of the ictus on the fermata – command of execution (coe); stop for the fermata (DON'T MOVE); upward gesture (pc); loop to the right and down (coe). If you want protracted silence at this point (*caesura*), wait at the bottom for a while, then prepare and continue. If you don't want that silence, don't wait at the bottom but keep moving through the ensuing ictus and into its rebound which will prepare the ensemble to get rolling again.

That last way is how the majority of fermatas are handled in most music, but this is a dramatic, interpretive choice. And in the former case, when I say DON'T MOVE I mean it. Why? Because we need to prepare the cessation of sound; a preparation is always upward, and if we have already migrated upward – which most do – we have used up most or all of the available space needed to perform the command of preparation. There's no more "up" left. (And don't tell me you need to "support the sound." That's nonsense.)

Speaking of no "up," there's a most important principle here: in order to move up, we must be down. So in general, keep your conducting forearm parallel to the floor; stay down and your preparatories for all moves will be immediately evident. The conducting hand must be "heavy."

Adjustable Wrenches

Gestures of Articulation include long (*legato, tenuto*) and short (*staccato, marcato*). To show **legato**, start at home base (with boing-boing) and reduce the height of the rebound. Now smoothly connect ictus to ictus, without emphasizing the ictus. Feel easy? It should.

Tenuto = *legato* to the third power. The connection from ictus to ictus present in *legato* becomes a *pull* from ictus to ictus, as though your hand were conducting the pattern in a vat of SAE 160 weight oil. And you must change direction very quickly. Feel easy? It shouldn't; it involves muscular intensity (in the deltoid) and actually moves ahead of the ensemble in time, though they will still move together because they adapt to this new paradigm quickly. *Legato* and *tenuto* involve manipulating the rebound.

Start at home base again with boing-boing (which is an upward spring, remember) and change the boing-boing to snick-snick by delivering the ictus very sharply and then STOP AT THE TOP OF THE REBOUND. The stop at the top says "short" to the ensemble. That's *staccato*. Feel easy? It should.

Marcato = *staccato* to the third power, so now change the boing-boing to BONG-BONG by again delivering the ictus very sharply, but DON'T stop at the top of the rebound (you heard it here). Not stopping says "marked" and we don't want to say "short" so don't stop. Feel easy? It shouldn't. It involves muscular intensity again, this time in the triceps. *Staccato* and *marcato* involve emphasizing the ictus.

Screwdrivers

The **Gesture of Syncopation** (GOS) is possibly the handiest tool in the box next to preparatory and release, and like them it has a lot to do with ensemble precision. All three involve "when." The preparatory says NOW you sing/play; the release says NOW you stop singing/playing; the GOS says WAIT, NOT YET, NOW.

Syncopation refers to rhythmic activity off of the pulse, not on it; for example an eighth rest followed by an eighth and then a quarter note. (um-pup-pah). Let's say the rest occurs on the third beat of a four-four bar. You do this: eliminate the rebound of beat two but use the full direction of that beat (WAIT, NOT YET), move sharply and quickly to the ictus of three (NOW), much like a *staccato* gesture (in many ways, a *staccato* gesture is a series of GOS's). Like *staccato*, you can stop (this time AT the ictus, not the top of the rebound), or, like *marcato*, you can continue with the rebound of three. It depends on the music. One is a slothead screwdriver, the other a Phillips head. Stopping is more powerful and emphatic; not stopping is more gentle and subtle. That's between you and the composer and your muse.

A foolproof way to ensure the precise delivery of that eighth note or, trickier yet, the second sixteenth following a sixteenth rest (um-pup-pup-pah), is to meld (see next page) for several beats in front of the event, and then deliver the GOS slightly early. I learned this from Rilling over 25 years ago. It really wakes them up.

Yet another principle is lurking here. With all other moves, we want the ensemble to react *on* the beat, thus the importance of the clarity and quality of the previous rebound. Here, however, we don't want them to react on the beat but afterwards, so we must eliminate the rebound. We can perform this gesture using the previous rebound (I often see it done that way) but it involves more work (the easy way, remember?) and probably more yelling from us when the ensemble doesn't respond with precision. No need to yell, just do it right. In fact, try it three ways with the ensemble: no GOS – a previous rebound – no previous rebound. And really listen. I'll wait here for you . . . . . . .Which was more together? Which was clearer to the ensemble? . . . .Told you.

Socket Wrenches

Melded and passive gestures are related (Green uses different terminology here, so try not to be confused: either will work. Or ignore Green. Or ignore me). They both involve conspicuous lack of rhythmic activity.

The **melded gesture** is used when you have a series of long or tied notes or both; say, two whole notes tied to a half note, followed by an untied half note. The idea is to meld through the long notes and ties (the whole notes and the half note), preparing only the notes which move (the untied half). The gesture itself is very similar to *legato*, but with an even flatter rebound than that of *legato*, and no ictus at all. You can help your ensemble's rhythmic sight-reading immensely by employing this from the very beginning. Again, try such a rhythm with and without the gesture. You'll see what I mean.

The **passive gesture** is similar to the melded except that there is no longer even a rebound. This gesture is the driest of them all, and shows only the direction of the pattern. It is most useful in recitative passages: helpful in *Messiah* and *The Creation* and absolutely essential in the Bach *Passions*. The rhythmic example above would now be quarter note (prepared), nine consecutive beats of rest (shown passively in the correct pattern), the final half or quarter (prepared). Taken to its extreme, say, four bars of orchestral rest in a recitative, this gesture would even remove all beats in the bar except the downbeat. All the orchestra would see is four downbeats in a row, and out of rhythm at least in my case. This latter is controversial – some would have you keep time and show the downbeats as they actually occur. Naturally, I'm comfortable with my own way and players never have a problem with it.

The passive gesture also comes in handy as an insurance policy at the initial attack of a fast piece, where there would not be time to accurately indicate tempo with only one upward move. Two clicks – sometimes three – are better than one in such cases. I don't think a whole measure is advisable, however, because the passive gestures can too easily transmute to active and become confusing. In general, two will do.

The key to the execution of both of these gestures is to keep any upward gestures very bland. Any energy at all in those upward moves (any "angle" on the Move, as I say to our students) and somebody might blurt, scrape or blow at the wrong time.

Breath indication is accomplished by a higher rebound than normal on the beat before, and then a stop at the ictus where the breath is to occur. Since we have stopped, even though briefly, we are now required to show a very quick preparatory for the next beat. This preparatory looks exactly like a subdivision of the beat and is precisely when the ensemble actually breathes; on the anacrusis of the beat.

Similarly, a *ritard* is shown by an exaggerated rebound of the beat before we want it to happen, followed by a gradual slowing down. Without that higher rebound (which says in semaphore, "yoo-hoo, lookee here") we will not have their attention and the *ritard* will not be together. We can buy another insurance policy for this gesture by employing the *tenuto* gesture (see page 27) after the semaphore signal. In this case, the ensemble will again be behind, but they will be together.

Accelerando, by the way, is also displayed by beating ahead of the pulse until the desired new tempo is reached. Then be with them again. This also works when ensembles are dragging behind tempo, and is the only recourse in performance because we can't stop and yell at them, now can we?

The Beat-Move Concept

Mastering the ten Moves above will equip us with 90% of what we need to convey our musical ideas to any ensemble. The final 10% has to do with any natural gifts which God may have given us, but doesn't depend on them because She has rather capricious ways of distributing Her gifts. (As my Viking ancestors used to say, "pray to God in a storm but keep on rowing." Or something like that. Closer to home, as Kuan-Fen Liu advised me not long ago when I was howling with anxiety and crippled by worry: "Don't *worry*, Dr. Dehning, WORK!" Those Asians sure know how to put me in my place!)

Moves need a proper setting to be visible, much like a jewel or a painting. The setting for a Move – that which is on either side of it – is nothing. (Well, not nothing, but almost. I have a penchant for hyperbole.)

As soon as our gesture indicates, say, *mf-staccato-presto* for more than two or three bars, that gesture is no longer conveying any new information to the ensemble. The Move has *become* a Beat through repetition and we are now merely Beating time. If we keep this up until a change in one or more of the performance parameters, the ensemble will ignore us, as well it should. We've become boring. What we should do is establish the parameters securely and then get out of their way and let them go, beating very small and maintaining only the *presto*; letting them maintain the *mf-staccato*. If we hear one of the parameters lapse, we can jump back in again and nudge the thing back onto the rails.

Seventy-three bars later, when things change to *pianissimo-legato-andante*, make a Move on the beat before and establish the new modes, Beat for a while, then go away until it's time for the next Move. Again, what we're doing is recognizing the principle of inertia and using it to our advantage (Don't you wish you'd paid attention in Physics? Did you *take* Physics?).

A lot of otherwise good conductors are TimeBeaters (strenuously flamboyant ones at that) because they simply cannot leave an ensemble on its own for awhile and let the members express their own musicality and creativity. Either because of ignorance or ego, they do not (or will not) drop the reins and let the horse (or camel, if you like) take them where it wants to go. I've learned that the horse often knows the way home at least as well as I do – sometimes better – and I occasionally see some interesting terrain (I don't know about the camel).

I learned this from Walter Ducloux (absent the cowboy and Bedouin metaphors) a long time ago. It is a very simple principle which we can see employed among naturally gifted conductors, but like all simple principles it can be difficult for those of us who have to work for a living to fully understand and effectively use. Succinctly put: 1) don't Beat for too long at a time (go along for the ride much of the time); 2) all Moves must be prepared a beat ahead of time; and 3) all preparations are up. You are now ready for the principle, which is this: **The Beat informs, the Move impels to action.**

Cleaning Up

Use of cues is often ignored by choral conductors, who tend to over-prepare their choruses into Automania. On the other hand, they can be turned into ostentatious fetish by orchestral conductors eager to display to the Board that they have memorized every one of them on the other. Cues exist for two reasons: substance (who has important musical events) and security (who will make a more confident entry knowing that "this is the time").

Because they usually see the entire score, choral singers need cues primarily for substance, although I'm stunned by how flummoxed sopranos can be by four bars of rest. The substance cue serves the primary function of letting the ensemble know who has what, so that the others can step aside and let them through. Substance cues are the immediate and inevitable result of the conductor's study of the score. Even though the ensemble sees the entire score, entries can be difficult if rhythms are tricky immediately before, and they might require a cue for security. I cued the chorus for this reason a number of times in recent performances of Stravinsky's *Les Noces*.

Because they see only their own parts, players have more need of the security cue, so spend time with the instrumental parts, especially the percussion and brass, noting who has long periods of rest or who has *ff* magisterial entries of material. Then mark these in the full score. I usually cue any *ff* entry and I always cue percussion and brass. I reckon you can't be too careful with anything that clangs, bangs or toots. And who enjoys counting 142 bars of rest? Not me. Pros will do it of course, but even pros enjoy knowing that they counted right. And if they aren't pros, we'd better be there every time in such cases. Finally, if a player misses any entry in any rehearsal, I will cue them every time, ever afterward, occasionally to their annoyance ("I'll *be* there, I'll *be* there"). Players are very proud.

Because the conductor's job is to help (more on that later), it may seem natural to try to get every cue, especially with players. This is not a good idea because cueing can consume the whole process, leaving little time for anything else. We must make choices. For me, the priorities, in order, are musical substance, long periods of rest, brass and percussion, tricky rhythmic entries.

How to cue is really simple but misunderstood. When I used to ask this question of undergrads at the University of the Pacific (UOP) for twenty years, their initial response inevitably was, "You point." This was their answer because they had probably seen too many orchestral conductors showing off. For me, that's the last method. I only use it if someone is very insecure, or if the entry is very dramatic and very loud – full brass at ff, for instance.

Most of the time, though, I use this: establish eye contact; then one beat before, turn the body and beat the pattern in their direction for a few beats. Simple, unobtrusive, clean. Sometimes I use the upturned left palm to invite folks in, or to make clear to the ensemble who has what. Most of the time, though, I cue with the eyes and a nod of the head. Or a smile.

Most conductors "mirror" too much with the left hand, and I am not without sin here, either (I am not without sin in most things on these pages, actually, which is in part why I feel I can write with a degree of authority on most of these subjects. Sin has a way of bringing things into focus). The left hand is an assistant to the right, period. It is used for the "ready" position at the very beginning of something, to hold someone out who may come in early – what I call the "opera cue" ("not yet, sweetheart . . .now"), and for the occasional pointed cue. Mirroring can be helpful in tempo changes and *ritards* and with orchestras to help the first violins because they are arrayed usually to the conductor's extreme left.

Primarily, the left hand should be used to shape phrase, help singers form vowels, turn pages of the score, and wipe the sweat off of bald brows like mine. Over-use reduces its effectiveness considerably – no need to kill a fly with a sledgehammer when a rolled magazine will do. The left hand is an emergency brake and a turbo charger – security only when we need it, power only when we need it.

Speaking of power, we come now to the conductor's symbol of it: the baton. But it is not a symbol, it is a simple lever – it can make things easier and more readily visible. Instrumental conductors use it primarily because they have players on either side of them and far to the back of the room or stretched way out in orchestra pits. Choral conductors tend not to use it because the entire ensemble is usually directly in front.

The majority of the time, most physical conducting is done with the forearm, with the elbow as the fulcrum of the pivot. A baton, because it is a lever anywhere from ten to fourteen inches long, allows this fulcrum to move forward to the wrist, making gestures more readily visible with very little physical movement. It also facilitates portrayal of delicacy because so little effort is required to move it. I like the baton. I use it with instruments, of course, but also with very large choruses, and, in a piece – regardless of chorus size – which is rhythmically very difficult and where "one" must always be very clear. I also use it in pieces like Brahms' *Liebeslieder* because nothing is more devilishly difficult to keep together than the twenty fingers of two pianists. I'd rather conduct twenty percussionists. Or twenty orangutans.

Oh, and the baton does not need to point straight ahead. (I disagree with Green here. Trying to keep the stick straight produces tension in the wrist, and tension is the last thing I want to convey to singers or anyone, for that matter.) Bring the right hand up, palm down (and when using a stick the palm must always be down because you want the tip down; do it wrong, see where the tip points), grasp the stick gently between thumb and middle finger, let the other fingers go where they want to. Notice now that the baton is at roughly a forty-five degree angle to the body, with the tip in the center of the body. Feel comfortable? Good. Everything physical about the conductor should feel and look comfortable.

A Last Thought and a Final Rant

What I have outlined here in regard to the craft is not the only way to do things. I'm not suggesting it is. We are all different and what works for me or someone else may not work for you. It doesn't matter so long as what we do works. Orthodoxy is not at issue here. If something does not work, however, I will say here what I say to experienced graduate students: I guarantee that what I suggest here will work (can't ask for more than that, can you?). I have been teaching this craft annually since 1968, have had some superb teachers over the years and have continued to explore this craft and improve my own practice of it. In short, I have made – and continue to make – a lifelong study of it. When strangers ask what I do and I tell them I'm a musician, they then ask what my instrument is. I tell them I'm a conductor (once we get trains and orchestras out of the way, I have to explain about choruses. See below). The first thing on my business card after my name is "Conductor, USC Chamber Choir." You betcha, by golly. And "conductor" should be the first thing on your business card if you draw a paycheck for doing it and are a member of ACCA.

In the old dictionaries, a conductor was defined as a transmitter of something: copper is a superb transmitter of electrical power. Musical conductors transmit power, too. They transmit the power of a fine composer's imagination to the fine people in front of them so that all may become better people through the process. Conductors are mere conduits, nothing else, though a number of megalomaniacs think otherwise. And if the music is not by a fine composer, why are we bothering to transmit it? Those are still fine people in front of us and they deserve white hot power for their spirits, lest those spirits flicker and wane.

That wasn't the rant. This is. You have probably heard that the technique for conducting an instrumental ensemble is different from that for a choral ensemble. Most often you hear this from instrumental conductors, of course – humble, self-effacing folks that many are. This proposition is founded upon pure, uncut male bovine organic effluent. Conducting is conducting. The visual technique is the same whether the ensemble is a community children's choir or the USC Symphony.

Certainly, there are different things to be aware of in rehearsal and in instrumental technique.   With an orchestra you must have fair command of C-clefs and transpositions, as well as some understanding of string bowing, brass and woodwind articulation, and tympani mallets. But if you can find your way around a word program or a spreadsheet, you can manage C-clefs and transpositions, believe me.

Choral conductors, on the other hand, have to be aware of the techniques of only one instrument. But that instrument is the most intractable, inaccessible, difficult instrument of them all to teach. And those singers usually come to us with less training on their instrument, often with scant ability to use that instrument to sight-read unless they learned piano or cello first. And you can't separate personality from the singer as you can with the player. My French horn was not an inextricable part of my personality – my voice is. Which is why when I blew a clam on the horn I would take the thing away from my mouth and scowl at it, much like a tennis player at his racket after a whiff or a net shot. When I sang a clam in the chorus there was nowhere to look but my shoes. Talk about humbling!

Finally, choral conductors must be confident in the pronunciation, basic grammar and vocabulary of at least six languages in order to effectively explore our six centuries of superb repertoire. I recently encountered a very experienced and proud and vain orchestral conductor who couldn't pronounce Latin, for god's sake. And not at all contrite about it either, 'cause he's the *real* conductor.

To a degree, we choral conductors have some approbation coming because many of us are not good, clear conductors, preferring instead to paint precious flower pots in the air which are indecipherable to all except ourselves, but especially to the ensemble, which hums merrily along despite the masquerade in front of it. "Incoherent" is often too kind a word in such cases. So fix it. Let's all become fine, clear conductors and shut those orchestral snobs up once and for all.

Because here's a flash from the front, folks: our job is far more difficult than theirs is. Compared with the tasks outlined above, clefs, transpositions, bowings, tongueing, and the like recede into the elementary and accessible. Once you learn 'em, you've got 'em. In contrast, I'm still studying languages and trying to figure out voices and singers.

The upshot? We should all be able to say this: I'll take any college orchestra for four rehearsals, give my chorus to their conductor for ten rehearsals, and we'll each choose our own repertoire.   In the subsequent concert, the orchestra will beat the pants off the chorus.

Every time.

Guaran-friggin-teed.

THE INSTRUMENT

I have spent all but five years of my entire professional career in collegiate choral music. Many would say I'm lucky, for obvious reasons (ask any middle or high school teacher, if the reasons aren't obvious). Others would mourn in sympathy because of the politics and the voice teachers and the low pay with which one must often cope.

And the turnover, too. Church, professional and community choirs replace only a few people per year. Every year since 1970, on the other hand, I have had to start over every fall with new personnel constituting 50-90% of the ensemble(s). Yes, even the "select" ensembles. Every year, in other words, I work with a "new" ensemble. And lest you think that I have worked only in the rarified atmosphere of perfect singers with perfect pitch, know this: from 1962 until coming to USC in 1992, I worked every year with choruses for which the only "audition" was a mirror held under the nose (if the mirror fogged up, they got in). So I know a few things about building an instrument – developing an ensemble, as it were – if only from sheer repetition and the instinct to survive.

Many of those things I learned from the ensembles themselves, especially the early church choirs from '62-'69. The last one of those wasn't bad but the first two were at times horrifying. However, I only know this in retrospect. Also in retrospect, I myself was horrifying, and I am grateful to those choirs for being so patient with me, for tolerating what had to be for them an often maddening combination of ignorance and insecurity, both of which were well-founded. I think it was four years before I could really *hear* an alto line, poor things (Janelle Steele at the break: "Bill, the altos are singing F# here, not G." Me: "Thanks, Janelle").

I am, in short, grateful to them for allowing me to make my many mistakes in relative obscurity and with relative impunity (Christian as they were). Those choirs were the anvils on which I hammered out my conducting and rehearsal technique. And this embodies another welcome, little-known truth which should give hope to anyone out there: we don't gain such techniques from working with good choirs, we get them from working with, well, less adept ones. (You can only improve your ear, however, with good choirs.)

There are ways to move the chorus forward along the continuum from abject to adept. These chapters about choral sound and how to improve it are the happy result of Charles Hirt's Choral Development class at the roots, my thirty-two years of teaching the subject to both undergraduates and graduates in the trunk, and forty years of working with the buds, leaves and blossoms of thousands of willing – occasionally grumpy – singers.

Vocal Fundamentals

Let's get one thing straight – and keep it forever straight – right now. The better the individual singer is, the better the chorus will be. Good singing is good singing, whether in recital or opera or chorus or shower. There is no such thing as the "choral" singer and the "solo" singer. Although it's true that many "choral" singers may never be thrilling soloists, the converse is not true. You give me a chorus full of fine soloists and I will give you one slam-bang chorus. I will expand on this topic in a later chapter, but for now the first sentence above seems so self-evident, so pungently logical, that for the life of me I cannot imagine why it is greeted with such surprise or spluttering almost every time I utter it.

Think about it. What is a chorus made of? When I asked Roger Wagner in a seminar at UCLA years ago how to get better sound out of the alto section, he said, "Get better singers!" This became known to ensuing generations of students in my classes as the Roger Wagner Method of Choral Development. It works, believe me.

But not all of us can use it all the time. What can we do when working with our "Y'all Come Choruses," or choruses where we are likely the only source of vocal instruction many in the ensemble will ever receive? We can work from sound principles of good, healthy *individual* vocal production. By far the overwhelming percentage of problems arising out of four of the six aspects of choral sound (intonation, diction, blend, and dynamic) have their basis in correct – or incorrect – *individual* vocal technique. Solutions to such problems lie in the voice itself. Absence of such problems in the great majority of singers in the chorus yields a chorus which, for example, sings with good intonation because good singers sing on pitch. I had no problems of intonation in 1996-97 with the USC Chamber Choir because almost everyone in it (including five doctoral voice majors) was a *singer*, regardless of nominal major.

The foundation of good vocal technique lies in both the brain and the body: the singer must think and hold the instrument correctly. As to thinking, the good singer is the best musician of all, because of all that must be on the mind before singing: pitch, sound, vowel, phrase, and breath. Instrumentalists can use muscle memory to help come up with pitch; singers can't. And players don't have to mess with vowels and sound. **The basic singing rules which must never be violated are think, open the mouth, breathe**. When I encounter problems in rehearsal, I check those three first.

Thinking is aided by good posture. Or is it the other way around? Is posture good because the person is thinking? Or is the person thinking because the posture is good? Does a well-dressed person feel better because he's well dressed? Or did she wake up tired and put on some of her best clothes in order to feel better? Tired of questions? Too bad, here's one more: what do you do just before you open the door for a meeting you're nervous about?

You stand up straight, take a breath and swing the door open with your head high, is what you do. The objective of good posture is readiness, mental as well as physical. And you see this mental readiness in the eyes, not simply the body. The eyes are not only the window to the soul, but to the will and the intellect also. Take a look at the eyes before a downbeat at your next rehearsal. You'll see therein who's not ready. The body merely manifests that condition. (Speaking of intellect, one of these years I'm going to select a chorus by having all applicants show me their I.Q. I'll walk down the line and choose the highest numbers I can find, without hearing a sound. I'll bet that would be a whopping good chorus. Ask Jim Marvin at Harvard about that.)

I need to mention the head here in regard to posture, since its position is critical to both resonance and phonation. The head is heavy – anywhere from fourteen to sixteen pounds, depending upon your opinion of yourself. If it is not balanced freely atop the shoulders ("floating," I say), the neck muscles will come into play to keep the head from falling down. We want those muscles free because they are very close to the muscles of phonation (below). We also want the head to remain level regardless of range because this will affect resonance. Many tenors, as we know, tend to reach for high notes with their chins, which is the worst thing they could do.

Respiration

Good posture, or in this case physical readiness, with the body in line from the hips up, also aids respiration. Muscles of respiration are major motor muscles, thus this vocal process is the most athletic of the three. Look at the platform diver just before the dive, or the gymnast just before the approach to the apparatus. There is a visible bodily uprightness of course, but more importantly, there is the presence of a marvelous balance between tension and freedom; of readiness. What follows immediately before the move?

A breath is what. In fact, as a basketball player I was known for my accuracy when shooting free throws. I used to win pizza and beer shooting them. My secret? A breath in both cycles – inhalation and exhalation – just before the shot, which soothed the tension in the mind and body, allowing the body to perform at its best. I wasn't as accurate with my jump shot in the course of fast action because I would often forget to breathe. I'd miss. Singers often forget to breathe, too. They miss.

Breath is different for the singer, though. With the body at rest, the rate of inhalation is roughly equal to the rate of exhalation: each takes approximately the same amount of time. For singing, however, the inhalation phase must be very quick, and the exhalation phase must last a l-o-o-o-o-n-g time in order to perform a phrase of any length exceeding seven beats (which is when most congregations want to breathe). Both phases of the respiration cycle require a "high chest" ("proud pecs," I call them; in some circles, it's "speakers front.") to be most effective. Both phases also require use of the abdominal muscles.

Correct, efficient inhalation is quick and silent. Quickness is accomplished with the abdominals: gasp and notice what happens. The abdominals pop out. What you don't notice, but what is happening, is that simultaneously with the abdominal expansion the diaphragm has dropped down, creating a vacuum in the pleural cavity. Since nature abhors a vacuum, air is literally pulled into the lungs, which expand to fill the vacuum.

This is nature's way of providing air in an emergency. Scientifically, then, those old Italians were correct: we don't breathe to expand, we expand to breathe. They were correct in another requirement for efficient inhalation (the open throat) when they suggested that we "drink" the air when inhaling. Drinking anything opens the throat. This helps accomplish the "silent" part.

I don't know about you, but every time I hear the injunction to "open the throat" I don't know what the heck that means. Shove something in there? Grab the sides of my neck and pull? Beats me. I never say it.

What I *have* found helpful is to suggest that the ensemble "inhale the vowel." This works every time, as far as I can determine, and strangely enough it doesn't appear to matter whether the vowel is closed, i.e., [i] or open [ɑ].

As with all matters dealing with vocal pedagogy in these pages, I list here only one example or device which works for me rather than a dozen or so. It's up to you in such matters to know or find others on your own if you need to. As I may have said at the beginning, this book is long on concept and short on example or detail, for which I have neither time nor patience in this format (my lectures are full of them, if you want to join us sometime).

Truth be told, *I'm* long on concept and often short on detail. I'm a concept kind of guy; I'm not always confident about the species of trees, but I sure know a forest when I see one. Adore it or abhor it, as you wish. And if you are unaware of the International Phonetic Alphabet (IPA), you are not only lacking a very valuable tool, you will be unable to fully comprehend much of what I'm going to say in this chapter. So get cracking on that.

Controlled exhalation is the more difficult part, involving the abdominals still, but now including the lower intercostals ("between the ribs") and the muscles in the lower back. To find these muscles, take a breath and hold it for a while, holding it at the belly and not with a closed glottis. Feel that? I try to ameliorate the difficulty of controlled exhalation by getting the mind to tell the body what to do. I do this a lot.

Also, when working with vocal matters in an ensemble setting, I try to tie vocal concepts into some basic human instinct, which is what I have done with the "gasp" above: the body *knows* what it needs to do in cases of instinct. The body can often *guess* what to do if the mind gives it a direct order or polite suggestion. What I said in regard to conducting applies here also: the body tends to coordinate when it knows what it is trying to say. So give it something to say.

In the case of controlled exhalation, what does the mind need to tell the body? **The length of the phrase.** And the body needs to know this before inhalation, actually. If the body knows the length of the trip, chances are good that it will take on enough fuel to get there. Keeping the abdominals out while singing (which tends to keep the diaphragm down) also helps considerably.

I said before that the process of respiration involved two phases. Physically, this is true, psychologically it is only half-true. Following inhalation is a moment of suspension, after which the singer initiates the tone "on the top" of the breath. I liken this to the tennis serve which I never mastered, thus gave up tennis. When you toss the ball up, there is a moment when the ball is moving neither up nor down, but is stationary. That's when you need to hit the ball and that's when you need to start the tone. With the voice, the belly muscles control this moment.

Then, following controlled exhalation, there is a phase of recovery, when the body relaxes in order to begin again. Sometimes, this recovery cannot last very long.

There are two ways to inhale: 1) slowly through the nose ("smell the rose, dahling"), which opens the throat and is slow; and 2) through the mouth, during which the throat must already be open and can be fast. The latter is often called the "catch breath." I call it the "second breath."

Both kinds of breath are necessary to effective breath control, but the second breath is the more critical of the two because there is usually less time for it and the singer must be very alert. Ever notice that your chorus's first phrase goes fine (time to breathe through the nose) but the second phrase dies after about four beats? This is normal, but like many things "normal" is often deplorable. The catch breath must be accomplished very quickly by pooching that belly out and keeping it there so that the second phrase doesn't die. In other words, the recovery phase of respiration must be extremely short. This Second Breath Theory is not well enough known among choral conductors, and is a key to effective breath management (you heard it here).

So, high chest, quick silent inhalation, long exhalation controlled by intercostals and abdominals. It's time to make some sound.

Phonation

The study of human psychology is divided into two camps, the Touchy Feelies and the Rat Chasers. Teaching methodology could also be divided into essentially two similar camps, the Psychological ("*think* or imagine this") and the Mechanistic ("*do* this"). Most good teachers use a little of both, and good voice teachers are no different. I mentioned before that the voice is the most difficult of all instruments to teach. This is in part because many of the important muscles doing the important work are involuntary; we have no conscious control over them. Even with respiration, the most important muscle – the diaphragm – is involuntary. We must trick that muscle into working by having its strongest neighbor, the abdominals, do most of the work.

The muscles involved in phonation are not only involuntary, they are tiny, and the nearest muscle neighbors in the neck and the tongue do nothing whatever to aid the process. On the contrary, they are often bullies and get in the way.

Here we encounter the other reason why voice is the most difficult instrument to teach: we have to teach almost entirely by getting inside the singer's head. The most important vocal process, phonation – when the vocal folds set up a vibration which produces the actual sound – is *beyond conscious control* except through the singer's imagination. The singer has to *want to* make a good sound (This has led to a degree of voodoo, cultism and witchcraft in the voice teaching profession. But more on that later.)

Those of us working with singers – especially in ensemble – don't have the luxury of saying "do-this," or things like "fourth position, first and third fingers, up-bow, thumb under," and the like. We are forced frequently to use simile, metaphor, suggestive images and phrases, and isolated, loaded words. We are most effective using "imagine-this" and "feel-this" and "think-this" instructions. This is especially true because we conductors don't have the capacity to work one-on-one in the privacy of the studio. We are often reduced to so many psycho-babbly idiots in front of God and everybody. (Some choral conductors rely almost entirely on permutations of personality, loyalty, entertainment, gymnastics, and cheerleading to get the job done. Many of these folks give good reason for our orchestral brothers and sisters to sneer at us.) Fortunately, modern research has given us enough information to know that some tried and true teaching techniques have basis in physiological fact and will improve the voice.

The key factor in the phonation process is the attack, or "onset of tone," as it is commonly coming to be called. It is the key factor because the tone is likely to continue the way it began and it's extremely difficult to change afterwards. Ever point a finger up when you hear the chorus flatting? Did it work? I didn't think so, and not only because no one is sure To Whom the Finger Points – it's simply too late. Before even beginning the sound the singer has to have a concept of the vowel, hear the pitch, and then *want to* produce a sound that might be pleasing to someone besides herself. Once that sound is out, it becomes part of history which, last I heard, is difficult to change.

The ideal attack is one in which the breath reaches the vocal folds just before they come together. If the breath gets there after the folds close, we will hear a glottal explosion that will be uncertain in pitch, ugly, and actually damaging. If the breath gets there too long before the folds close, the tone will be breathy but at least this does no harm. Of the two sins, this is the one we can live with, because the air must be started first. (This has basis in both physics and physiology, but you're going to have to look up the Bernoulli Effect – the one that keeps aircraft aloft – if you want to know more.)

Because of the need for air flow at phonation, most voice teachers will use "liquid" consonants in their initial exercises: mee-may-mah. I also found light *staccato* exercises most helpful to teach attack because they involve the belly, because many attacks must start on a vowel, and because they are difficult to do wrong. Try it like Dracula: ah-ah-ah (wrong). Try it like a cynical coed: h-h-h-ha, h-h-h-ha, h-h-h-ha (wrong). Now try it right (in the middle of the wrongs). See? Difficult to do wrong. (I get a lot of mileage – and giggles – out of doing things wrong, by the way. People can not only feel the difference, they can hear it. And people aren't stupid. They want to do things right, they often just don't know the difference between right and wrong. So show them.) With groups that I had to "teach" a lot, I did *staccato* exercises at every rehearsal. With the USC Chamber Choir, I still use *staccato* occasionally, but not as exercises. Rather, I have them sing whole portions of some pieces *staccato*, thereby capturing two, maybe three butterflies with the same net. And *staccato* helps to set up and instill that moment of suspension which is so critical to the accurate, healthy attack.

Resonance

When I became a horn player, John Robbins gave me a battered Olds single F horn. I played that miserable thing for three years, and it wasn't until I got to UCLA when Clarence Sawhill loaned me a Conn 8-D double Bb horn that I had any real idea what a difference an instrument could make. Wow, was that double horn easy to play! Whole new worlds opened up with that snazzy little thumb trigger! The main difference between the two instruments, of course, was in the shape and length of their resonance chambers. The quality of the sound and the ease with which it was produced depended to a great degree on the size and shape of that resonator. The same is true of the voice, except singers don't have to run out and buy a new instrument to improve the quality of the tone. The resources to change that tone at will lie – literally – right in their very own heads. What they need to do is adjust the cavities of the mouth and throat to form vowels with a consistent tone of uniform quality. This is easier than it may sound, but only with desire.

Resonance, like most things, lies in a balance, this time between "space" and "ring." Ring is sometimes called focus, ping, buzz, core, zing. It is the so-called "singer's formant." (In case you haven't grasped this already, terminology is one of the more controversial and difficult aspects of vocal pedagogy. We all have to muddle through as best we can, depending on the audience at hand.) Resonance became immediately clear to me in William Vennard's vocal pedagogy class a long time ago. He sang the following to the tune, "The Farmer in the Dell":

> The singer's in the nose,
> The singer's in the nose,
> Hi-Ho, the derry-o
> The singer's in the nose.

He sang the above in a nasal twang (too much buzz). Then he sang it again, but this time, "The singer's in the *well*," with a somewhat muffled, woofy sound (too much space). Finally, he sang "The singer's in the *bell*" with a balanced, "good" sound. (Maybe this is where I learned the effectiveness of doing things wrong deliberately.) The effect is immediate, anyone can do it, and I have used it every time I have to teach a new group what "good" tone can sound and feel like and do it quickly.

Focus is the result of efficiently functioning vocal cords. If the cords vibrate close together, with good breath balance, and with only enough opening between them to allow the tone to be produced, the tone will tend to be focused; it will be clear and not breathy. If focus is not already present in a voice, it is the aspect of resonance that is most difficult to achieve because it takes the most time. It needs to be nurtured in the individual lesson, because it involves the use of muscles that are easy to abuse.

Too much focus in the voice is the domain of Appalachian banjo pickers and too many telephone receptionists. In singing, it is usually achieved with exercises concentrating on the closed [i] and [e] vowels, starting in the mid-range and moving out. It employs the upper resonating chambers of the nasal passages, hence the expression "singing in the mask."

Space, on the other hand, is much easier to achieve, involving the second of the three basic rules of good singing mentioned on page 40:

open the mouth. The important question is, what do we mean by that? We mean that the jaw swings comfortably down and back, the tongue is relaxed and low, the soft palate is raised, and the larynx is bobbing low and loose in the throat, even in the upper register.

What the foregoing conditions have done is to create maximum room in the oral and pharyngeal cavities, which are the only ones that resonate the vibrations set up by the larynx. The nasal cavities are not directly involved, meaning that the soft palate must be up. There is a *sensation* of being up there, but it is not real. You can demonstrate this for yourself by singing a tone while pinching your nose shut. If the tone changes quality, the soft palate is down (tsk, tsk). Now lift the palate and sing . . . .Hear that? The point: the design of the resonator can (must) only be changed by movement of jaw, tongue, palate, and throat (lowered larynx). The lips put the final color on the sound, but that's for later. Exercises to achieve space usually employ [ɑ], [o] or [u] starting in the upper part of the range and sighing – sometimes literally – downward.

But how do we achieve those optimal conditions in the oro-pharynx? Another good old instinct, the yawn, is one way. We mammals yawn because the body has an immediate need for oxygen, and when the body really needs something it tends to have its way with us. In this case, it opens the throat, closes off the nasal passages with the soft palate (the nasal passages move air too slowly for the body's current needs; this is no time for yoga), relaxes the tongue down and out of the way, and lowers the larynx. Bingo. The body gets its fix of oxygen and you are ready to sing. Caution: the ideal singing conditions are present only at the *beginning* of the yawn; during the yawn itself they are distorted beyond all musical use. So start a yawn, but don't finish it (unless you're listening to one of my lectures or sitting through the *Ring* cycle).

Placement

In the intangible nature of working with voices, this topic may be the most vaporous. There is nothing physical whatsoever we can ask the singer to do; we can only ask that the singer feel, imagine, or think, whichever works. Placement exists entirely in the singer's imagination yet it is very important to free, clear resonance. I'll tell you what it means, then I'll tell you what I do to help achieve it in ensembles.

Again we're talking about balance. The tone must not be imagined too far "back" in the cavity (common in overcompensating basses and altos), nor too far "forward" in the mask (common in some tenors and sopranos trying for more projection). The former can produce tone which resembles that of a frustrated lower primate; the latter can produce a tone that would peel paint. Neither is beautiful. (I wish you could hear me make these sounds. I've heard them so often in my career that I can reproduce them with hilarious results. Truly. But I'm still not going to make a CD for you.)

The tone must be imagined to be a floating bubble centered two centimeters below the soft palate in the dead center of the mouth. Raising the jaw or lowering the soft palate would pop the bubble (nudging the tone too far forward); raising the back of the tongue would pop the bubble (trapping the tone too far back). Told you it was tricky.

I have often gotten the right placement by having the singers inflect all sound upwards, over the top of the head, not off the bottom of the chin. Sometimes we use hand motions to help induce this sensation. (Voice teachers *always* use hand motions to induce this sensation.) If that doesn't work, I have them say "oh" as if they've just heard a joke to which they know the punch line – bored, in other words. That's wrong because the sound is dull ("too low in the mouth," I tell them). Then I ask them to say "oh" as if they've just heard some juicy gossip about someone they don't like very much – interested, in other words. This usually works because the sound now has that "high arched resonance" vital to well-placed tone. At least the sound is now interested ("keep it high in the mouth," I say).

I have to keep reminding singers to constantly produce "interested" vowels all the time, every time, and I will stop if they don't. I will not accept a bored or dull sound. Out of tune, imprecise, yes, wrong note, even. Dull, no. Evil is not the enemy of the good, mediocrity is (you heard it here). Dullness needs to be a punishable crime.

Registration

You may hear a lot of theories about how many registers the voice has, but physiologically there are only two. As the voice rises from the low register to the higher (with a quite thick approximation of the vocal folds), it will eventually reach a pitch at which the folds "flip" to accommodate the higher pitches (to a very thin approximation of the folds, along the edges). No matter how much higher the voice goes, there is no further change. This change in operation is called a lot of things, but I'm going to call it the "break."

In common, real-world parlance, though, there are three registers to the voice: chest, middle and head registers. With regard to registration, the object of all good voice teaching is to achieve a full-toned, even timbre on all vowels, from top to bottom of the voice, effortlessly, and without physical sensation. In untrained singers, the break is quite noticeable, especially in male singers. In natural, or trained singers, the break is hardly noticeable, if it is noticeable at all.

Most of us have to work with a lot of untrained singers. The most helpful thing I can say here regarding registration is that the use of the falsetto in the male voice is invaluable in achieving the higher range, and indispensable in helping tenors evolve from an airy falsetto toward the true head voice. I will also say that the upper register requires more space in the female voice, and more forward placement, or more forward vowel modification, in the male voice. Both genders require less space in the chest register.

Putting It All Together

Ready? The singer's instrument is an entire body with a low center of gravity, from the elastic quadriceps, up to the firm gluteus maximus, up to the free, loose abdominals, maintained by proud pectorals and loose shoulders. Up, finally, to the crowning achievement of the singer's brain encased by the head, which is level and loose. When we start this formidable engine – the connection of the breath to the vocal folds at the right time, with a raised palate, open throat and relaxed jaw – it is called *coordination*. As I said before, singing is an athletic activity fueled by an active brain that has deep creases.

When you see or hear folks doing all that, sign them up. Great singing may be the finest thing human beings can do, other than write poetry. If you don't hear and see all that I have described in the previous paragraph, help them along the way as best you can in the time you have with them. Great teaching may be the second best thing human beings can do.

THE ENSEMBLE:
VOCAL CONSIDERATIONS

Now we take all of these individual instruments and make a composite instrument that will become greater than the sum of its parts. The principles that govern good individual vocal production must now be applied to a group of generally willing people. If a sound working knowledge of the voice is systematically applied to a group of singers, they will have good tone; they will have a fine choral sound. If the tone is bad, there is a vocal fault which must be determined and corrected. This is always, naturally, a work-in-progress (sorry about the buzz phrase). It is never perfect, but it is the *sine qua non* of our daily work. What do we want this new instrument to do?

Aspects of Choral Sound

We want it to sing with a uniformity of vowel sound. That's blend. We want it to communicate a language with intelligibility and grace. That's diction. We want it to sing true to some relative standard of melodic and harmonic pitch. That's intonation. We want it to sing in musical sentences with accuracy and agility. That's precision. We want it to sing with an equal quantity of sound within and between sections. That's balance. Finally, we want the tapestry this instrument weaves to have color and variety. That's dynamic.

Blend

Blend is possibly the most over-rated aspect of choral sound. Certainly it is the least understood, so I'm going to start with what it is not: it is not balance. Even many professionals confuse blend with balance. Balance is quantity of sound; blend is quality of sound. There are three ways to achieve it, historically and in current practice.

Western choral sound is historically most influenced by the musical practices of the Roman church. That music was sung by choruses of men, or by choruses of men plus boys with unchanged voices. Do most male voices have wide vibratos? Generally, no. Do the unchanged voices of boys have vibratos at all? Generally, no. Choruses composed of singers with minimal or no vibratos sound blended. A

vibrato is the individual character of a voice which is a result of
efficient, free production in a post-pubescent human; it is characterized
by an easy oscillation slightly above and below a pitch. Natural, gifted
singers have this quality built in. It can be acquired with training, also.
Remove that oscillation and combined voices will sound blended (and
terrifically in tune, by the way, which is one reason that most good,
young choruses, and most good European choruses have such fine
intonation. But more on that below). Remove that individual
characteristic and all voices will tend to sound alike, thus blended.
That's one way to achieve blend and is the so-called "straight tone"
approach. Sound simple? It is, and it's also fast and I sure like the
intonation that results, but I don't recommend it. I don't take the easy
way out on this one.

If we don't want to make the voices sound alike, we can take another
easy way out and make all vowels sound alike. We can do this by
darkening all vowels, shaping them toward [ɔ] or [o]. This gives an
ersatz maturity to the voice and you can still hear it in some high school
choirs whose conductors like a richer, more mature sound than might
otherwise be available in younger voices. These conductors generally
work from the [u] vowel and derive all other vowels from it. It works
because what we're doing here is removing the upper overtones from
the vowels, and it's those upper overtones which give vowels their
individuality. Remove those upper overtones and the vowels will tend
to sound alike, thus blended. (That's why [u] is the easiest vowel to
blend – it doesn't *have* any upper overtones.) Sound easy? It is, and
it's also fast, and I have used it in some clinical and festival situations
where time matters more than morals, but again, I don't recommend it.

Here's what I do recommend and here is what blend truly is: everyone
singing the same shape of the same vowel at the same time, which is
another way of saying "uniformity of vowel sound," but more
precisely. Sound easy? It's not. It requires continuing refinement on
our part of exactly what we want to hear for specific vowels, as well as
continual education of our singers ("brainwashing," if you like)
regarding what we and they consider beautiful sound to be. (And
beauty is what we're after. If it ain't pretty, who wants to hear it?) We
have to be fascinated with the sound of languages, if not their grammar.
Make a hobby of phonetics, if you haven't already.

I shouldn't say it isn't easy, because in principle it really is. What I mean is, this method of achieving blend takes time; we can't be in a hurry. I used to be delighted with "Y'all Come Choirs" if we got five vowels together by the end of a semester. If you're in a hurry, choose a bunch of singers without vibratos (which a lot of conductors do, especially Europeans – one of these years I may try it myself, just for fun) or darken all of the vowels.

What do we gain in return for this time? The gratitude (at least the grudging tolerance) of any voice teachers we're involved with, and most importantly, a vast palette of color which the other two methods can't even approach. A more interesting sound, in other words. Blend can be bland. For many conductors, blend is merely an attribute, not a goal. Ever notice how your ear gets bored with the sonority of those straight-toned choirs after about twenty minutes, no matter how excellent they otherwise are? It's like listening to a harpsichord recital (maybe not that bad). It drove my voice-teacher-wife nuts on our German sabbatical. Why bore people? Why drive my wife nuts? Concentrate on the vowel because (you heard it here) the sound is the vowel. Highlight that one.

Other Factors

Individual vocal color can adversely affect blend, but rarely, and even then only in the smaller of choruses. If we work with a select choir of less than twenty, we should select those voices carefully based on the distinctive properties (color first, then size) of each voice. Otherwise the only alternative is to have some singers (probably sopranos) do something vocally unnatural in order to produce the ensemble sound we hear in our head. This paragraph does not apply at all to larger choruses, or to professional ensembles of mature, highly trained, excellent singers, no matter how small.

The acoustic of the rehearsal hall can affect blend. It's more difficult to sing the same vowel as someone else is if you can't hear it. If your room is dry, get them in a circle occasionally, or have the front row turn around and sing toward the back row. Ask some good singers in the section to sing the wrong shape of the vowel; they'll hear the effect instantly. (Never ask poor singers to do it wrong, for obvious behavioral reasons.)

Don't confuse balance with blend. Balance is quantity: singing the same volume as others in the section, or in balance with other sections. Someone singing *forte* while others are singing *piano* doesn't necessarily have a problem with blend; she does have a problem with balance. Or brains. Blend is dependent upon balance, not vice versa. The reason that blend improves with "scattered" seating (see the next chapter) is that the balance does.

Diction: Enunciation

Think about it, what's a singer singing 99% of the time? A vowel is what. And even with the other means of achieving blend, it cannot be really done without unified vowels. The question is, which vowel? That choice depends to a great degree on pronunciation, which is the first component of diction. We have to determine how a word ought to be pronounced according to some generally accepted standard, either a dictionary or educated personal preference. I prefer [ɛ]nvelope, for instance, rather than [ɔ]nvelope. But no matter what I prefer, dog is pronounced d[ɔ]g, not d[ɑ]g, and I don't care if you are from Chicago, you're going to do it my way. The other two components of diction are enunciation and articulation, which follow in great detail right now.

Enunciation is the component of diction that deals with vowels. To "enunciate" is to care for the clarity and purity of the vowel. Careful enunciation is a nice, polite, unnecessary thing in everyday speech and it's a helpful thing in solo singing, but it's absolutely critical to blend in choral singing. If you don't give a flip about blend – and many don't – the following discussion of vowels might still give you some food for thought, maybe a few useful concepts or tools. At least some interesting cocktail hour chatter.

I'm going to try to get a triangle out of this machine. Hang on a minute. . . . . Aw, to hell with it. Draw your own bloody equilateral triangle. Draw it on the next page.

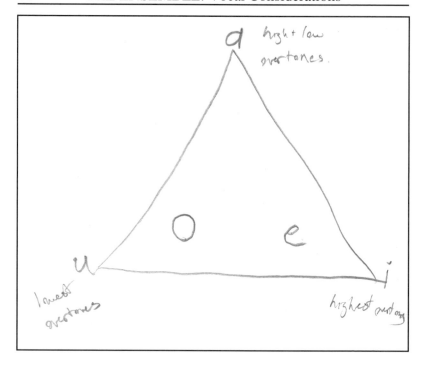

At the top put an [ɑ], at the left angle put an [u] and at the right side angle put an [i]. Now in the middle of the left side put an[o] and in the middle of the right side put an [e]. These are the primary vowels, the so-called "pure" and so-called Italian vowels. I prefer "primary" because I get to play some more with my metaphor of vowels = colors. In fact, I see vowels in color. Also voice parts: I like brown altos, gold sopranos, orange tenors and hot red basses – if the latter get blue or brown, they go flat. (Choral sound itself is almost tactile to me. I can *feel* it. But that approaches The Weird and I'm not going to talk about it anymore.)

Just as we can derive all other colors by mixing the primary colors of red, blue and yellow, so it is with vowels. Except with vowels we have five primary colors and we only need to mix and come up with about eight more to sing most of the Indo-European languages quite intelligibly and gracefully. (Notice I said "about." I'm taking the easy way out again.) And just as with colors, there is an almost infinite variety of shades, so it is with vowels, except we have to choose one shade that we prefer and want to hear in general, or in a specific piece for purposes of mood.

The Vowel Triangle

Each vowel has specific acoustical properties. In some respects, each vowel is an "instrument" unto itself. The [u] has overtones near middle C, [o] has them at C1, and [ɑ] has them at C2. Thus [u] sounds "darker" and "lower" than [ɑ]. We could surmise from this that if we keep moving around the triangle, the [e] and [i] vowels will have higher overtones and we would be correct; [e] has overtones around C3 and [i] has the highest of all at approximately C4. BUT, the vowels on the right side of the triangle have not just one set of overtones, but two. The [e] vowel has a second, lower set at C1 – in the same place as [o], and [i] has a second set at middle C – in the same place as [u].

Triangular Implications

The perceived rise in pitch as we move around the triangle from left to right is unconsciously part of human knowledge and language. Note how the following sequence of words appears to rise in pitch: "moan, shout, yell, scream"; "roar, squawk, squeal"; doves "coo" and chicks "peep." I repeat that [i] and [e] have two sets of overtones, with [i] having both the highest and lowest set; [u] and [o] each having one set, with [u] having the lowest. The [ɑ] vowel is at the apex and has one set of overtones partaking of both sides of the triangle, that is, it shares acoustical properties with both the [u] and the [i].

Stated more colorfully, a properly resonated, deep-orange [ɑ] is derived by mixing the red of [u] and the gold of [i]. Another way of looking at all of this technical information is that [e] = ([o] + a somewhat faint higher overtone) and [i] = ([u] + a very pronounced higher overtone). This latter ersatz formula of mine contains strikingly important information, possessing enormous implications for the sound of an ensemble.

The [i] can be unsurpassed in ugliness if [u] does not serve as the "base paint" for it. Say the word "we," which is a glide from [u] to [i]. Now say it again and let the [u] fall out of the sound as you move to [i] – raise the jaw, in other words. Hear that? Ugly, ain't it? An [i] is ugly without the lower overtone of her beautiful sister, [u]. No one wants to date her alone; they gotta come in pairs. So bring a friend and buy two corsages.

The [ɑ] is in many ways the Master Vowel (or Mistress Vowel, if you want). It is the nearest to the Original Human Sound, "uh." It requires the least modification of the sound produced by the vocal folds. Start repeating this primordial glottal grunt, and gradually relax the larynx while simultaneously lowering the jaw. Open your mouth. What you arrive at finally is [ɑ]. In acoustical fact, [ɑ] = a properly resonated "uh." (Speaking of acoustical fact, none of the foregoing information is the mere opinion of My Own Exalted Self. This is physics, *mes amis*, not philosophy. If you want more, the best source for much of this is William Vennard's excellent *Singing: The Mechanism and the Technique*. For a more pragmatic, everyday approach based on these principles, I recommend James McKinney's *The Diagnosis and Correction of Vocal Faults*. McKinney was one of Vennard's earliest students.)

Further Triangular Implications

Some more experiments, OK? (I wish I'd had this much fun in chemistry and physics labs. I guess I'm in the right business.) With your properly resonated, yawn-sigh [ɑ] as a starting point, move down the left side of the triangle, forming vowels on the way. The lips move on this side, and they move a lot. They protrude, they don't pucker. The jaw should not move. Do the experiment again with a finger on your Adam's Apple (no, not Eve's Apple; Eve's is harder to find, ever notice? Besides, we went and ate Eve's Apple and have been in a lot of hot water ever since). Note that the Apple tends to drop as you move to [u]. This is good, and is part of the reason that the vowel has the richness it does.

What you have done is made the aperture of the vocal tract smaller with the lips, thereby removing higher overtones. Did you move lips only and let the jaw just hang there? Good.

Start again at the top with your properly resonated yawn-sigh [ɑ] and this time move down the right side of the triangle, forming vowels on the way. This is a bit trickier than the left side because the jaw wants very much to move and we must not let it. It's the back of the tongue that should move and it doesn't move much at all. Mere desire is enough to achieve these vowels.

What you have done is make the vocal tract smaller with the back of the tongue, thereby producing higher overtones. Perform this same experiment again with a finger on the Adam's Apple. Note that the Apple wants to rise as you move toward [i]. This is bad, because as the larynx rises we lose sight of [i]'s prettier sister, [u], and [i] is left all alone out in the rain, becoming ever wetter and uglier. Keep the jaw down and the soft palate up, which will help the Apple to bob lower in the vocal tract. For heaven's sake, bring [i] in out of the rain. Fluff up her hair a little.

Above all, do not smile on this side of the triangle, at least with the lips. Smile inside, at the back of the opening. Never smile at [i] with your lips. If you do, she gets other ideas and becomes nothing but a tawdry little tart. She starts chewing gum and saying things like, "I don't *think* so." Keep those lips loose on this side of the triangle; they have nothing whatever to do with the sound over here. Do your best Nixon imitation, if you can remember him. (If you don't want to remember him, I understand.)

Basic Implications

What those last paragraphs have done is work along the base of the triangle, rather than its sides. We've already seen that we should always move from left to right, that we must incorporate [u] into [i]. This is a one-way street, though. If we go the wrong way on it, crashing the yellow of [i] into the blue of [u], we will smash up the [u] utterly, in fact producing the mangled Germanic and Gallic mixed vowel [y], the so-called "umlaut" vowel. This vowel is green and may be one of the uglier sounds in Western languages.

Let [u] remain blue in all languages, but especially in English. (This may be only a regional accent endemic to the West Coast – "e-e-e-uuu!" – but it drives me nuts; straight up the wall. I hear that sound in an [u] and I start looking around the room for my Scandinavian relatives, launching into bad imitations of the Swedish Chef.)

Secondary vowels are derived from one of the primary ones, but are a shade more "open" or "closed" than the primary. These adjectives, open and closed, are describing what's physically happening to the resonating chamber or its aperture. We can now fill out the triangle completely. As I go through this, you write it in your triangle.

Open [u] a little, you get [ʊ]; open [o] a little, you get [ɔ]. The most open vowel of all is [ɑ] and you arrive at the top of the triangle. Go directly to [i] at the bottom. Open [i] a little, you get [I]; open [e] a little, you get [ɛ]. You can now do some more note-taking and make columns of open and closed vowels, so you are sure to understand thoroughly where they belong on the spectrum were we to break the triangle at the left base angle and straighten it out in a flat line from [u] stretching all the way to [i]. Back to the triangle. Inside the triangle, midway between [I] and [u], write [y]; open that vowel a little, you get [Y]. Midway between [o] and [e] write [ø]; open that vowel a little, you get [Ø].

You have now filled in the sounds necessary for Germanic and Romance languages, but there are two necessary for English that I haven't mentioned, the "bad" vowel [æ] and the "dull" vowel [ʌ]. The "bad" vowel's place on the triangle is below [ɑ] on the right side. The British have no problem with this vowel, but Americans can really make it scrape metal. They must make sure to give it a lot of room in the mouth without migrating all the way to [ɑ]. Let the British sing "dahnce," it sounds affected when we do. Sing "d[æ]nce." It's a perfectly legitimate sound as long as you're not from New York or Jersey. Or Chicago.

The dull vowel's place on the triangle would be right under the [ɑ] on the left side. I rarely use this vowel, especially with less-experienced singers, because it can be really "ugly." I prefer instead to all but ignore it and open this vowel to [ɑ]. Say the very common words "up, love, come, but" both ways and you'll hear what I mean. I'd much rather they sing like Dracula ("I lahve to keess your nack. Cahm weeth me. Ah, ah, ah." *Sesame Street* lives on in my rehearsals!)

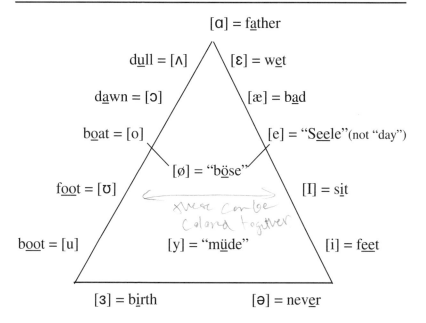

[ɑ] = f<u>a</u>ther

d<u>u</u>ll = [ʌ]   [ɛ] = w<u>e</u>t

d<u>a</u>wn = [ɔ]   [æ] = b<u>a</u>d

b<u>oa</u>t = [o]   [e] = "S<u>ee</u>le"(not "day")

[ø] = "b<u>ö</u>se"

f<u>oo</u>t = [ʊ]   [I] = s<u>i</u>t

b<u>oo</u>t = [u]   [y] = "m<u>ü</u>de"   [i] = f<u>ee</u>t

[ɜ] = b<u>i</u>rth   [ə] = nev<u>e</u>r

Enough Geometry

I have found this investigation of vowels and their properties useful on a daily basis for my entire career. It's not just for us academic types, *amici miei.* I have never lectured an ensemble on them, of course, because there isn't time. I consistently have a blackboard on hand, however, and manage to scribble IPA symbols on it in every rehearsal, no matter what language we're using. When I don't have time to even scribble, I am referring constantly to open and closed vowels. There aren't that many vowels, really, as we've determined, but getting them right according to our understanding and taste is immeasurably helpful vocally, for ensemble diction, for blend, and even for ensemble intonation.

At USC in particular, with its very large body of international students, and where I work consistently with Koreans, Taiwanese, Japanese, Bulgarians, Hungarians, Poles, and one Jordanian in the room, we would be in *caca profunda* without such tools. Yes, English may be the common vocabulary in use, but its correct pronunciation rarely is, even among the native speakers from Green Bay, the Valley and Houston. Thank you, Jesus, for the IPA! And blessings on Jehovah for open/closed classification of vowels! And (what the heck) praise to Allah for the vowel triangle and for His people, who also gave us the zero, Arabic numerals and higher mathematics, as well as the best, most beautiful rugs in the world!

Consistency of vowel color, or uniform vowel production, is easier and more accessible if we realize that the well-rounded tone, regardless of vowel, contains in some measure both the yin of the [u] and the yang of the [i] (or is it the other way around?) All vowels should sound as if they all come from the same family and live in the same house.

Yes, [i] will be more brilliant than [u] but the difference needs to be moderated. We have to bring [i] down a peg now and then because she wants to show off her glittering high overtones all the time. We must keep in mind, too, that it takes very little movement to travel down the right side of the triangle, but it takes a lot of lip activity to produce clear, closed, well-placed [o] and [u] vowels as we journey down the left side.

If the singers have a well-rounded [ɑ] and do not allow the other vowels to depart too far from it, then the singers have solved the problem of uniform vowel production and we have solved the greatest part of our blend problem. And we did it solely with sound individual vocal technique.

Vowel Modification

Speaking of show-offs, sopranos have a unique problem. Look again where the overtones of the vowels lie on the keyboard. Now think of the customary soprano range and tessitura in all but popular music and arrangements. Can you see why the upper set of overtones in [i] are so easy for her to produce? Then extrapolate a bit and realize that on her higher pitches – upper staff and above – it is impossible for her to produce the *lower* overtones of [i] and [u], *because* the *fundamental pitch is already too high.*

In the upper range, the soprano is unlikely to get any tones too deep: quite the opposite is not only likely, it is painfully common. She must modify closed vowels to open ones as pitch rises – rather than [e], she should sing [ɛ], for example – and at the extreme upper end of the range she is justified in singing *any* vowel she finds comfortable. Probably [ɑ], the most open of vowels. Let the men and altos sing pure, closed vowels in such cases if you want the audience to understand what you're singing. The soprano *can't* because – no voodoo, no Method here – it is *acoustically* impossible (not uncomfortable, *impossible*) for her to do so. Acoustically. Sorry to use so many *italics* here but this is an *especially* important point. Sopranos are the *first* thing the listeners hear (sometimes it's *all* they hear, but that's for later), because the overtones of their instruments are so *penetrating*, as are the higher pitches that are written for them to sing. Sopranos can *really* be a problem so they have to get the sound right. By "right" I mean not only powerful (which many of them feel is the *raison* for their *etre*), but beautiful, too. Beauty is one of the two main reasons to be alive (the other is Love. Unlike Keats, I find Truth somewhat more elusive and variable according to culture, but you handle it your own way).

I have nothing against sopranos; I married one and begat two more. I love and worship sopranos, especially when they are good. But altos are my buddies, good or not.

Speaking of buddies, men must modify vowels, too, but in exactly the opposite way. I don't know about you, but I've managed to notice that despite all the Women's Movement and the Men's Movement have tried to do to get the genders to dress and think alike, there remain abundant differences between men and women.

In addition to the fact that men have larger larynxes, thereby singing at least an octave below the women much of the time, another difference is in the manner of their vowel modification, which is from open to closed – the other way around from women. Hence as pitch rises, it is helpful for the male instrument to gather higher overtones for both clarity (important) and ease (critical). A male would modify an [I] to [i], then, for example.

Truth be told, I generally prefer men to sing [i] rather than [I] regardless of range or pronunciation. It clears the fuzz out of the bass voices and helps the tenor considerably through the break. Tenors will often just "ride that buzz" right on up with hardly a whimper, indeed with the aplomb and arrogance for which tenors are justifiably famous. So in the line, "Come with me under my coat..." from Barber's *The Coolin*, I ask the men to sing, "Cahm weeth me, ahnduh my coat. And we weel dreenk our feel ahv the meelk ahv thah white goat, or wine, eef eet be thy weel." If they merely speak this it sounds like a bad Spanish accent, as in a recording I heard of Placido Domingo singing a John Denver song like this: "You feel op my sensess" (think about it). But men singing this way in general can produce a glorious tone on secondary vowels that might otherwise lack luster. It can sound really virile (which most women like, if that still matters).

Singing Secondary Vowels

Speaking of lackluster, secondary vowels have a tendency to distort too much from the primary, thereby lacking vivid color. I must repeat what I said above about movement from vowel to vowel: it doesn't take much at all, especially on the right side of the triangle, but on the left as well. Relax the tongue only slightly from [i] to achieve [I], for example, or relax the lips only slightly from [o] to form [ɔ].

The point is to relate secondary vowels closely to the primary, or relate the open to the closed, if you prefer. Most American choirs, in my opinion, would be far more colorful if they would re-discover two very important secondary vowels, [ɔ] and [ʊ]. To my ears, they invariably sing "bought, caught, song, long" far too close to the [ɑ] vowel, too open in other words. [ɔ] is a brother to [o]; [ah] is only a cousin. Similarly, another color missing from the American lyrical palette is [ʊ], as in "foot, look, book, would, should." This is a very rich, dark sound which is a fraternal twin to [u], and again, is usually sung too open. Its color is purple and purple is the color of passion. So if you don't sing this vowel, you sing without passion (sorry). Some are aware of this problem and go too far, singing the [u] instead, thus rendering a decent imitation of a Slavic accent ("Varry gude, beeg boy!"), but if sin you must, I would rather hear it the Slavic way.

I'm not alone, either. On my first sabbatical in 1980 I spent a lot of time observing and chatting with the superb British choral conductor,

John Alldis, as he worked with both his amateur and professional choruses. He asked his singers to sing all languages – but especially English – as if the vowels were Italian. A good idea, because contrary to prevalent common wisdom, Italian does have open vowels besides [ɑ], they're just not easy to hear because they are so closely related to one of the "pure," closed ones. This is true in both song and speech and is the reason that Italian sounds so much clearer and brighter than say, Spanish. In an Alldis-coached ensemble, this produced a richer, warmer sound than I usually heard in my six months in the country. British choirs are excellent but can be quite clear and chilly. Maybe because of unheated churches and cathedrals. Or those wet, miserable winters. Or residual Viking blood from three hundred years of pillage and you-know-what.

Diphthongs

Speaking of coupling, we come now to a topic common to English and German but named after Greek words: *di* = two, *phonos* = sound, therefore, "two sounds" in English. (This word is almost always mispronounced; you need both *h*s. Or both *f*s, actually. English is the most polyglot language because it's been married, invaded and you-know-whated so many times. Makes it difficult to learn, but gives it a vocabulary unparalleled in its precision and variety. Nowadays, of course, English is doing the invading and you-know-whating around the world, much to the horror of primarily the French. Talk about historical irony!)

I'm going to use English for demonstration, not German, and refer those of you who want more than is here to a book which is still one of the finer books on the subject (certainly the most humorous), *The Singer's Manual of English Diction*, by Madeline Marshall.

Diphthongs are composed of two vowels; the first called "dominant" and the second called "vanishing." They come in three classes, Primary, Secondary and Neutral, named for the characteristic vowel on which each is based. I'll just give a few examples of each and then come straight to the point.

Examples of Primary diphthongs are **night = [a+I]**, and **now = [a+u]**. West Coast females and Southwesterners of both genders usually pronounce the second one as [n+I +æ+u], thus rendering a decent imitation of a hungry cat. It is without question the most distressing diphthong for those of us who believe that English can sound beautiful, whether spoken or sung.

Examples of Secondary diphthongs are: **joy = [ɑ+I],** and **day = [ɛ+I].** I didn't make a mistake there at the end. In English the latter is not a pure vowel but a diphthong. English speakers do not use the pure, closed [e] when speaking their mother tongue. (Sorry, "parent" tongue, I guess I should say, but how do you mothers feel about that?)

Neutral diphthongs have a Primary or Secondary vowel as the dominant one, but are so-called because they have the "neutral" vowel, or schwa [ə], at the end and because they involve a final "r." Examples are: **air = [ɛ+ə],** and **sure = [u+ə].** (Is it necessary for me to tell you how Americans often mispronounce these? Naw.) The common word "our" (and "hour") is actually a **triphthong [ɑ+u+ə]** and is usually mispronounced by omitting the [u], thus rendering a rhyme with "are." I have never satisfactorily solved this problem or maybe have stopped trying because I don't consider it critically important in the Grand Scheme of Diction, I guess. Who knows? Maybe you can come up with a solution, if you consider it important.

The most important thing when singing diphthongs is to sustain the dominant vowel until the last possible millisecond and then move quickly through the vanishing vowel. How about some Cole Porter? Give a brisk quarter note to each dominant vowel: "N[ɑ]-[i]t[æ]-nd[ɛ-ɛ-ɛ-ɛ-ɛ-ɛ]-i[u][ɑ]-th[ɑ]-u[ɑ]n." In popular style, of course, this is often sung, "Night and d[ɛ-i-i-i-i-i-i-i-i]," but you should never sing it this way, regardless of style. Listen to Frank Sinatra, he does it right.

In the lyric above we encountered two diphthongs which are called "glides" because we skip over the first vowel, which is usually dominant and sustained, to the second one, which usually vanishes but is now sustained: you = [I+u], and one = [u+ɑ]. (The last one is actually [u+ʌ] if you want to be perfectly correct, but I'm brainwashing you.)

Marshall calls such things **"inverted"** because, as in a glide, dominant and vanishing vowels reverse functions. Common examples are: few, new, dew, Tuesday, tune, and stupid. If pronounced correctly, the first four have a lot more flavor than otherwise, and the last one has plenty of bite. But except for "few = f[i+u]," these are commonly mispronounced as "noo, doo, Toosday, toon," and "stoopid," thus rendering a decent imitation of a mouth-breathing knuckle-dragger with non-opposing thumbs. (Or my beloved German and Norwegian immigrant grandparents, but they had a good excuse, as do all immigrants. Neither set of grandparents ever spoke anything but English in my presence, by the way, because they and their children and their grandchildren were Americans now, and poor as they were and hard as they worked, it must have beat the heck out of what they had formerly known, by yiminee. Make of that what you will. I had to learn German on my own, long after Wilhelm and Gertrude were dead.)

Summation for Singers

The individual singer must do two things to enunciate well: simplify and modify. He must mentally and quickly break words down into their smallest and/or dominant component and sing the right vowel (simplify). *She* must shape any closed vowel more toward the open one as pitch rises. *He* does roughly the opposite (modify).

The individual ensemble singer must do both of the above, plus one more: (s)he must do the utmost to assume the same color of vowel as others singing the same words at the same time (unify).

Simplify, modify, unify, these three abide all of the time in choruses. And there is no "greater of these" this time. They all matter equally.

Diction: Articulation

Let's throw some spices into this stew of vowels, shall we? That's one way I look at consonants, which is what vocal articulation is all about: they enhance the flavor. Without consonants, vocal sound of any kind – but especially choral sound – can be bland, amorphous (my daughters and I have a cooking mantra: "no salt, no taste; no fat, no flavor"), not to mention unintelligible, which is the main, generally acknowledged purpose for consonants: so folks can understand what we're singing about. In the worship service this is indispensable. In other settings and for other reasons it may not be so important, at least in itself.

Consonants are used for **pedagogical purposes** also, because they tend to bring the sound forward and into the mask, providing clarity to the tone. I find this often helps with those flat, muddy basses, as well as altos with hair on their backs, who can also sing flat. In such cases, I don't yell at the offending parties for being flat (they don't mean to be), I ask them to be more explicit with explosive consonants and usually the pitch is corrected. If the offending parties forget next time and the problem recurs, then I yell at them.

More important to me as a musician, though, is that consonants **display rhythm**, give a zing to the vocal line, hence also displaying precision in a chorus. Unlike other instruments, we can't articulate rhythm by tonguing reeds and mouthpieces, whanging on goatskins and Turkish metal, or scratching horsehair across dried cat intestine. God knows we don't bang little felt hammers into a bunch of tight strings. Poor us, all we have is the wherewithal to do things all those people wish they could: go straight to the hearts of the listeners with a *legato* line that is the envy of every instrumentalist. And that *legato* line shimmers with natural vibratos that winds and strings have to simulate with shaking jaws, quivering bellies or palsied left hands and God knows what all.

We've got The Word, with all that it can imply on a human level. This is the most important purpose of consonants to me: they give **emotion and drama** to the flow of sound based on vowels. That's what consonants are all about. I don't really give a round rodent's bottom that your words are intelligible if they aren't *saying* something...about the desolation in the sonnet; about the frivolity in the ditty; about the comedy and drama of the human condition. Vowels alone can't do that. You need consonants to do that. Example straight ahead.

Say the word "love," lingering a long time on the first consonant. Make note. Now say it lingering on – and emphasizing – the second. Two different emotions emerge almost without intention, right? The first may have been something like love, but the second was probably more akin to lust. These are two different emotions. (Well, maybe not to men, they often can't tell the difference. Or just don't care if there is one.) Imagine what you could do with intent. The possibilities are as limitless as are the colors in vowels; more important, as limitless as the range of human emotion. Thus consonants are not mere bothersome noise, they are very effective, versatile tools for the expression of musical thought.

Classification of Consonants

People specializing in languages and phonetics classify consonants according to where the sound is stopped, because that's what consonants tend to do, stop the sound (or vowel). They use words like "labial, dental, guttural," and the like. It's fascinating (there isn't much I don't find fascinating, come right down to it) but we don't have time for that here. I got a more practical classification from Charles Hirt, who put them in order of their ability to enhance or disturb a vocal line. I'm going to also put them in order of disturbance, from least to most, and then give you a practical concept or two about each class. I must admit here that I don't really know all of the correct IPA symbols for consonants, and for the classic reason – at least classic in my case – I haven't had to. I'm the same as anyone else, learning what I must when I must. (My first daughter didn't learn to cook until she got married. Didn't have to. I didn't learn to cook until my second daughter was born. I had to, or lose my wife. I changed diapers, too, for the same reason. No, just kidding. I *liked* changing diapers.)

"Liquid" consonants are least disturbing to the vocal sound. These consist of [m, n, l, and ng]. Really, though, they are **Voiced Sustained** consonants (they carry pitch) whose other brothers and sisters are [v, th(e), z or s (as in "pleasure")]. If they precede a vowel, they should be sung on the same pitch as the vowel. If they follow a vowel, they should retain the pitch of the vowel. Handling the pitch of resonant consonants – especially initial ones – in this manner has much to do with good intonation.

Remember, too, that initial resonant consonants take time so they must precede the beat. We want the listener to hear the vowel on the beat because it carries the most sound. Otherwise the sound will be perceived as late, even though the consonant was sung on time. Say and conduct the word "zoo" placing the consonant on the ictus: we don't hear the vowel until the rebound of that ictus. Say and conduct the word again, except start the consonant at the top of the initial rebound, before the first ictus. There. Now the vowel is heard at the ictus. This principle of *sustained* consonants preceding the vowel is especially critical when singing with instruments, whether piano or orchestra. The chorus will sound behind if it is not systematically applied.

Voiced Explosive consonants are [b, g, d, dj]. These must be dispatched as quickly and emphatically as possible. I sometimes also use them preceding neutral syllables when basses start to sink in pitch, or if they are swallowing the tone (ba-ba-ba, da-da-da). Such consonants help give frontal focus, relax the lips, and can free the tongue from being swallowed.

Unvoiced Sustained consonants are obtained by taking the pitch away from their noisier cousins. We then get [s, f, sh, th(ink)]. Since they can take as much time as their noisier cousins can, they too should precede the vowel, lest the sound be perceived as late. The sibilants [(s, sh)] are often troublesome at releases when, for some reason unknown to me, singers want to hold on to them forever. Anybody know why? Enlighten me, please.

Unvoiced Explosive consonants are also derived by removing pitch from the voiced [b,g,d,dj], giving us [p, k, t, ch]. Except for [p], these are rarely difficult to hear, since they contain as many high overtones as the sibilants. In fact they are often overdone to the point of farce.

They should almost never be louder in dynamic than the vowel to which they are married (I know, I know, some vowels have two spouses). Choruses and their overreaching conductors often use them to show off their "good diction" with them. I have heard more than one *pp Kyrie* spoiled by a Killer K . And more than one *ppp* ending ruined by a Terrific T. Balance, moderation – fine words representing fine principles. Only in *Carmina Burana* can they be ignored. (I have not done this work, nor have I wanted to. I let my replacement do it on my first sabbatical, though, so the kids could have a rousing good romp with it, God love 'em. Audiences love it too, often interrupting with applause (talk about High-Loud-Fast Syndrome!); professional choruses use it to make money, in the manner of *Messiah*; professional baritone soloists have it memorized. It is really quite easy for the competent conductor to conduct and one can show off like crazy in front of all that sexually-aroused-Neanderthal noise, acquiring instant Possessed Maestro status. I don't know what's wrong with me. Huh. I do find *In trutina* from the work to be ravishingly beautiful in all ways, especially when my wife sings it, but it's only about a minute long.)

The R-R-R-s

The initial [r] can be a real asset, because it is a Voiced Sustained consonant, but among Americans of mid-western origin and elsewhere, internal and final [r] can really put a painful laser beam into the ear. There are three kinds of [r]: American, which the English use only at the beginning of a word (as in "rose"); rolled, which is used only in languages other than English; and flipped, which is only used in English between two vowels in the high register. I only have time for the American [r] in English and I'm going to cut straight to the chase, omitting character development and dialogue.

Never sing [r] before a consonant or at the end of a word. And for the one and only time in this book, I do mean never. *Never.* To do either is to produce a sound second in ugliness and annoyance equal only to that produced by the omnipresent Urban Cricket, the car alarm.

Before a consonant, omit the [r] entirely and sing the vowel only. Which vowel to sing is not always evident by simply looking at it, as I discovered early in my career with church choirs. Words like "Lord" and "born" were not difficult once I discovered that the vowel was [ɔ], not [o].

But words such as "earth, birth, world," and "word" can be tricky for many Americans, most of whom are unfamiliar with the "stressed schwa," [3]. (True for American men especially, who don't want to sound like affected Oxford dons. Have them rent some movies with Sean Connery in them; if the sound is good enough for that stud, it's good enough for anybody.)

It's just fine for Americans to speak these English words like George Bush II (I would hope in more complete phrases), but we should sing them like Elizabeth II. (Speaking of "good enough" and Bush II, who was once governor of Texas, some time ago a former Texan high official was opposing bilingual something-or-other in that state, which has many Mexican immigrants. He did so by saying that if English was good enough for Jesus, it was good enough for Texas. True story.)

At the end of a word, [r] is replaced by the unstressed schwa [ə], for example in two more of my Favorite Church Choir Words, "ever" and "never."

Finishing Up

In all of music making, singing is unique. The vocal mechanism is not only used as a musical instrument, it is also – primarily, actually – a means of spoken communication. Instrument Mode requires constantly – and consciously – maintained optimum conditions for the production of tone based on vowel. Speech Mode involves making a rapid series of symbolic sounds that are in continual flux and essentially noisy because of the consonants, especially in Germanic languages. And consonants can destroy good singing tone, in particular that of females in the high range ("We don't *care* about intelligible, we want to hear *beautiful*," I remonstrate with Nordic firmness).

Conscious of this fact, I tend to ignore consonants in the early and median stages of the learning process of a given repertoire, except for those few used for specifically dramatic or emotional purposes. Once the multi-colored conveyor belt of pure, free vowels is running smoothly and the pitches are learned, I drop the consonant pebbles on near the end, providing the definition, life and polish necessary to sophisticated music-making of any kind. I train them first to sing on the vowel.

I didn't always do so. I learned it when my wife used to give some lessons at home while I was in the kitchen cooking and had no choice but to listen. So many times, she would ask the student to sing without consonants. The sound was better. Not being a complete Teutonic blockhead, I tried it with some choruses and found it to be a successful learning device. I also discovered that over time the groups were developing a rounder, richer sound. An over-emphasis on consonants in the early stages will tend to produce a whiter, shallower sound. This is of course because consonants also tend to bring the voice forward. Indeed, they are often used explicitly for that purpose. Even by me. Duh.

Homework

Now do yourself a favor. Fetch an English dictionary and look up the definitions of "articulate" and "articulation." How do any of those definitions apply as used in the second chapter, *The Score*? What is the difference between articulation in that chapter and in this one, if any?

There's only one right answer to these questions, and it's yours.

THE ENSEMBLE:
CHORAL CONSIDERATIONS

Intonation

You should know this, coming right out of the chute: if I had the
answer to this problem and could copyright it, I'd be rich, famous and
worshiped worldwide. I'd be hiring the best singers and players I could
find, paying them like royalty – including life-long insurance and
princely pensions for them and their children – and rehearsing and
performing like crazy. I'd even hire the audience.

None of the above is the case. I'm just one who works at it as best I
can without ruining the fun by making an obsession of it. And until
forming a semi-pro group in 1986 and then emigrating to USC in 1992,
I worked with singers just like yours. It was a revelation to me in 1986
that, as I said earlier, really fine singers sing on pitch in a chorus. If for
some reason they lapse from good pitch, they know it and fix it. The
conductor doesn't have to do doodley-squat. (We disbanded after ten
years, in part because I was tired of traveling north all the time, but
more important because at USC I was sometimes working with singers
who were almost as good, lacking only *bassi profundi* like Jim Heiner
and Rich Colla.)

Listen to those Scandinavian (including Finnish and Baltic) and
professional European choruses sometime (recordings won't do it for
you, you have to be in the room). What really strikes you is the
remarkable, crystalline intonation. Robert Shaw's Festival Singers was
the only American chorus in my experience that was in the same league
with such ensembles.

Clarification

But back to reality. Even at USC, where three out of our ten ensembles
in my ten years have been truly championship teams (in education,
three for ten ain't bad), I still have to wrestle quite a bit with problems
of pitch and intonation. The last two nouns are often used
interchangeably and that's OK. I make a distinction in ensemble work
just for purposes of clarity. If the group flats a half step, the pitch is

down. If one section or the entire group is starting to flat, I yell "pitch!?" because self-awareness is needed. Pitch is macrocosm; the big picture.

On the other hand, if the sopranos are not in tune with one another, or if the tenors are not in tune with the altos (who are always on pitch and in tune), I yell "listen" because group awareness is needed. Intonation is microcosm, is internal. And know what? Sometimes the pitch has dropped slightly over a period of time and we occasionally don't know it because the intonation has been so good. Maybe pitch affects intonation but the converse is not true. (Good singers always know it, though, even the ones without perfect pitch. They feel it in their voices. I feel it too, but in my deltoids and hands...and actually, I never "yell." Seriously. In the cases above, I don't have to, anyway, because the fault is usually occurring during a passage characterized by the Low-Soft-Slow Syndrome. All I have to do is say it.)

If you-all don't notice the pitch moving slightly off-center, you can be sure the audience won't either, including professionals who may be out there (as I have proven to my immense relief after performing for ACDA conventions). Pitch is relative. That is not so of intonation, and therein lies the problem. Any listener will forgive many things of a chorus, but poor intonation is not on the list. Next to a wrong entry, poor intonation represents the greatest distraction from the artistic experience we're trying to provide, and even your half-deaf Uncle Fred can hear it: "Say, Rabi, wasn't there some of them there sour notes coming out from time to time?"

Extrinsic Causes

This class of causes is most well-known, thus receiving the most blame for problems of pitch and intonation, after Mondays, menstrual periods and male menopause. This is unfortunate, because there is often little we can do about them but complain. Don't. Try to alleviate or remove the problem if you can. If not, just be aware of it and accept it. An excuse is what you *don't* want it to become. (In athletics, this is called the "Loser's Limp." A sprinter is only meters from the tape, sees he can't win and suddenly pulls up lame with a "limp." He doesn't want anyone else to know what he knows: he was giving it everything he had but he still was going to get torched by that speedy little sucker in lane three. There's a conductor's analog to this, which I'll touch on later.)

Weather. Do I have to say any more? Would it do any good?

Size of ensemble. (I think you may have heard it here.) Regardless of the quality of singer, pitch seems to suffer in direct proportion to increasing group size. This is entirely a matter of group psychology. The individual singer often feels less important, or lets Suzie do it, or feels he can hide and lip-sync at the suggestion of an unsympathetic, possessive voice teacher (UPVT) who hates choral singing on general principles.   This is especially true in matters of musicianship, particularly sight-reading. I repeat: regardless of the quality of the singer, if you're one of only four or five singers on that part (two or three, if double chorus or full *divisi*), you produce, by golly.

And not out of fear of the conductor, either, as the aforementioned UPVT may think. Karen Schrock produces for the best of all reasons: personal pride. She wants the other sopranos to know that she will do what she needs to do to help everybody succeed; mind your own business, thank you. (As you might have surmised, I have little empathy with the whole Self-Esteem Movement. You want self-esteem? Work your bummy off and do something right; self esteem will then be just around the next corner. Go get it.)

Temperature in the rehearsal room, especially if poorly ventilated and/or overheated, makes a big difference. Cooler is better. Only the sopranos will complain. Make them do some jumping jacks.

I worked for thirteen years, four months and twelve days in a WWII Quonset hut situated in California's central valley where late autumn and spring temperatures were at least in the high 80's, often breaking three digits in the afternoon.   (We got a new building in January, 1986.) The only cooling in the room was a noisy 1950's vintage evaporative cooler, known ubiquitously as a "swamp box." Both choruses – one with 40 voices, the other over 100 – rehearsed at three in the afternoon. I felt like a shepherd in a sheep shed on many occasions. (Talk about sweat!) Did this Lutheran lad, raised in the arctic winters of northern Minnesota, fresh from the blazing autumns and snows of upper Michigan, complain in front of the ensemble? Not once. No excuses. Was the rehearsal pace brisk? You betcha. Do you see why my eyes glaze over when I hear people complain of such things?

Poor rehearsal time can have even more adverse effects than temperature. In order, the best times are late morning, early afternoon, evening. Most professional choruses rehearse from 10:00 to 12:30, which may be ideal. The worst is early morning. I spent many pre-dawn hours buzzing around northern California in order to be at a clinic with a high school chamber choir, in part as penance for my vastly easier professorial schedule. Many of these groups started as early as 6:30 a.m. because it was the only time available for such "unnecessary" ensembles in a crowded schedule. (As is often the case in American culture, the few busiest, best and brightest are punished for being so.) I have nothing but admiration for those kids and their conductors. I stand humble before them and do anything I can to help them anytime they ask.

Poor acoustic can have minor bad effects in the learning stages, fewer as the music is mastered. Very dead rooms will promote flatting pitch in slow, soft music, sharping pitch in fast music, whether loud or soft. Intonation can also often suffer in such rooms for reasons previously mentioned. Very live rooms promote flatting because things can sound so good with such little effort that the singers stop putting out the effort, becoming less active and alert. Sharping in live halls can occur if the ensemble becomes enamored of its own sound and tries to make even more of it, forcing the voice. A moderately live room is best, the higher the ceiling, the better.

By way of summary, let's go back to that high school choir in northern California. Here they come at 6:30 on a foggy Monday morning into a cold, carpeted room that has ten-foot ceilings covered with acoustical tile, as are the walls. They are absolutely stoned with physical and psychological fatigue from lack of sufficient sleep, and all but vocally incapable of speech, much less song. The only extrinsic thing they have going for them is their small size, plus a fine, dedicated conductor who loves them and music. That's enough, apparently, because they're awfully good. They're not squirrelly under such conditions, that's for sure.

Fatigue in the ensemble straddles both classes; sometimes it's outside of our control, other times we can do something about it. If the fatigue is physical, singing lighter, quicker things helps, as does softer *staccato* rehearsal of the score in question. It takes strain off the body by enlivening the brain.

Vocal fatigue is engendered by singing too long, of course, but also by rehearsing too long in either dynamic extreme or in the high range. I work from *mp- mf* in the early stages, which seems to aid stamina, and I rehearse down the octave a lot if the problem is pitch or rhythm. I also use light, *staccato* syllables preceded by voiced explosive consonants in such cases, but fatigue will only get worse if we don't change the vowel from time to time. I alternate among [u,o,a,e].

Psychological fatigue means they are tired of the passage of music, the piece itself, or me. I know when this sets in because their eyes start to cross. In the first two cases, I follow one of my own rehearsal commandments, Thou Shalt Know When to Quit, and reach for the parachute. In the last case, I try to forestall it by varying my vocabulary, rehearsal routines, pace, facial expressions, gestures, and clothes. When those fail – and they inevitably will – I have someone else stand in front of them for a while and conduct. This works. They're always glad to have me back, even if the other conductor was undeniably excellent; Rilling is excellent, but he ain't me, is he?

Intrinsic Causes: Flatting

With extrinsic causes, we must either alleviate or be aware and accept. With intrinsic causes, we must discover as many of them as possible and devise solutions or approaches for them. Causes for flatting are many. Most colleagues I know have more trouble with this than sharping because it is so closely linked with vocal production, especially vowel and breath. So, as usual, *cherchez la voix, mes amis.*

I'm going to list what I have learned through my own studies and experiences to be main problems, but it is not a complete list. In most cases, the solution is obvious: "don't doo dat." If it is not obvious, I don't always list a solution, either because I don't have a foolproof one or it may just work for me, or it would take far too long to go into here. In our classes, we take the time. This is not a class, though, and my phone number is unlisted. I will say to search first in the Vocal Trinity of Brain-Body-Breath. Chances are good the solution is in there somewhere. Ready? OK, then: "Into the valley of death rode the six hundred . . ."

A few vocal causes are already listed above. Here are some more that will almost ensure flat pitch:

- Constriction in tongue or jaw ("sing hot consonants" – quickly out of the mouth lest they burn; use "yo-yo" or "ya-ya").
- Swallowed vowel; sound too far back (same as above)
- Wasting breath at the beginning of the phrase, so it goes flat for lack of fuel at the end – this is a biggie.
- The break areas in the voice: soprano, d-f; alto, b-d, tenor, d-f, bass, b-d – this is also a biggie (see next one, too).
- Chest voice pushed through the break (they must learn this: foot off accelerator, clutch in, shift gear. Only the most natural and/or well-trained of singers have automatic transmission).
- Glottal attack too low in the throat (*staccato*, humming; sometimes the conductor can induce this with stiff, harsh, high gestures – don't doo dat).
- Placement too low in the mouth, producing bored vowels (humming, "sing through the eyes").
- Suzie sings [u] while Brie sings something more like [y] – ain't no way those two sounds can be perfectly in tune; same thing happens when [o] is called for and the basses sing their classic "morff" while tenors sing their classic "ya-a-a-a-æ" – vowel unification is critical for good intonation in unison or homophonic passages, or within a single section in polyphonic ones. "Critical," the man said, and it better be a good vowel or not even unification will help.

Technical Causes: Flatting

Technical causes arise from the printed page, the music itself. In many cases, the solution to them lies in our awareness of them, listening for them and consequently pointing them out to the ensemble if they arise.

- C-related keys, when sung unaccompanied, tend to migrate downward because important pitches, i.e., the scalar (step-wise) seventh or harmonic (think chord) third, may lie in the break area of one or more voices. This includes F, G, and all three related minors. Who often sings the third in C? Tenors, quite often, maybe even sopranos. What is the melodic seventh of F and G? See what I mean? If not, there's more coming. Transpose these keys up or down *ad libitum* if sung unaccompanied. B and Db major stay right at home in my experience. Experiment. (If you have to sing sixteen or more bars in one of these keys while the piano or orchestra takes a break, then pray devoutly at the beginning of the passage, and if it comes home on pitch burn a candle in gratitude that evening because you have been once again favored by the gods.)

- Repeated tones, whether immediately in series or a constant return to the same note, can have a tendency to wear on the singer psychologically – "oh, that note. *Again?*" ("Renew your relationship with that note at each encounter," I say calmly in shrink-speak, "don't take it for granted.")

- Ditto the above with sustained tones, especially if the sustained tone is in a lower voice and a voice above it has a descending passage ("Stay home, altos," I say, and they do).

- Ditto the above in suspensions, particularly if a half-step is involved. The bottom preparatory note – especially if tied across the barline – wants to sink as the dissonant note grinds against it ("Stay home, basses," I say, and they don't).

- Descending half-steps are almost always flat (practice descending chromatic scales. Heck, practice descending *quarter* tones, for that matter).

- Descending minor thirds are usually flat; in the bass voice, "usually" becomes "always."

- Ascending whole steps can be flat, especially if more than one, and especially if they reach the tri-tone (practice ascending whole-tone scales).

- Ascending perfect fourths need to be very enthusiastic ("Here Comes the Bride!") or they will be flat.

- Ditto ascending perfect fifths; double-ditto for both intervals in the bass line.

- The melodic major seventh must always be sung higher than imagined, even if a bit sharp to the piano – the piano is tempered,

singers and other man-made instruments are not. The same is true
of the harmonic major third – a C in an Ab major chord is a higher
pitch than the C in a D dominant seventh (the piano doesn't care
about such things).

• Beware the LSS (Low-Slow-Soft) Syndrome (the chorus must
maintain forward motion, the conductor must, too).

• Chords involving the major seventh: the seventh tends to go flat if
in the soprano, more often a root in the bass may fall down to the
seventh itself, making a D major seven an F# minor, for example
(rehearse this without the root, then add it – easier to hear that
way).

• Chords involving the minor second: rehearse without one of the
dissonant notes and then add it. Make sure that the dissonant note
is balanced, and that everyone hears it and enjoys it; it should hurt
good.

Bass Causes: Flatting

I've made some unkind references to basses so far in these pages, not
all of them entirely deserved. (Actually, I've taken a few shots at
sopranos and tenors, too.   Also conductors, voice teachers and
harpsichords. Is there anyone out there who hasn't been offended yet?
If so, be patient. I eventually get around to everyone, including My
Own Sweet Self, as you may have noticed already.   Only altos are
immune from my blasts.)

More than any other voice, the bass wants to be a quarter tone flat and
a quarter-pulse behind. To a certain degree, the latter characteristic is
inherent in the nature of the instrument itself; it's heavier, the folds are
longer, and it just takes a bit longer for the air to get moving, to
"speak," (not unlike contrabasses, contrabassoons and tubas).

I think the tendency to be under pitch is in part cultural, and again not
entirely their fault. Everyone *expects* them to be the dramatic "heavy,"
the bourbon-drinking bullyboys of the bunch. So they are. If we want
them to wear the black hat, they will. *Con mucho gusto.* This assumed
machismo carries over into the vocal production quite easily so they
want to produce a more testosterone-soaked sound than they are really
capable of, eschewing high overtones in the sound, which makes pitch
flat. I also suspect lower pulse and metabolic rates, but I have no
empirical evidence for this.

I pay special attention to the bass part, for one thing because they sing all those fourths and fifths and roots. I may be ignoring one or two other sections on occasion but my ear is always on the basses. Sopranos can be flat and the ensemble will often stay right to home, but if the basses go down the entire ensemble goes with them. No life jackets either. They are the acoustical foundation of the choral sound, much like the tuba in a brass quintet. All members of the ensemble must be aware of the bass part and find their places in the overtones it generates.

Sharping

Ever struggle forever with flatting pitch in a piece or passage, only to have it be dead center in performance? Boy, I have. (Why didn't they do that in the first place, anyway? No wonder I'm skinny and bald.) The ensemble was excited because some people were out in the hall, everybody knew their stuff, the conductor walked on stage looking pretty good for a change, and for once they were going to get to go through everything without stopping, praise the Lord. Excitement of that nature causes tension, the good kind, so pitch was good.

Tension is what causes sharping. Tension is a physiological reaction to a psychological state. Here are some of those states, most of them not good:

• Worrying about staying on pitch.
• Trying too hard in rehearsal or performance.
• Beware the HLF (High-Loud-Fast) Syndrome; sopranos and children's voices, especially, can really inhale helium and rise quickly – "Up, up and away . . ."
• Rigid, stiff, forced conducting motions (they tend to sing what they see, at least we hope they do).
• A frenzied rehearsal pace.
• Tension caused by the conductor losing his sense of humor and values under the pressure of performance (more about this in another chapter).

For me, a rise in pitch of no more than a quarter tone does no harm in unaccompanied music; it adds a little lemon to the butter sauce, in fact.

Rhythm and Pitch

Robert Shaw said that 75% of intonation is rhythm. He also said that "sloppy rhythm and poor intonation make a pretty smooth couple." (Shaw was an extremely brilliant, possessed man with a wonderful sense of humor. If you haven't read *Dear People* by Joseph Musselman, treat yourself. You'll be inspired.)

I observed many of Charles Hirt's rehearsals with the USC Chamber Singers during the years I was a student there. I wasn't a good enough singer to be a member. Talk about voices!   And yes, it's the same group it is now my pleasure to conduct, but I changed the name in 1997, after five years with them. I asked Hirt's permission to change it and he said, "OH HELL, YES. I DID!" – I use capitals a la John Irving's *Owen Meany* because Hirt was on his second Scotch and could truly rule a room with that voice and the magical things that issued from it, including his laugh. That man was a lion on the hunt in all ways: eyes, chest, hair, movement, roar, you name it. Especially in rehearsal.

Not once did I hear him even mention intonation. The air in the room put me in mind of the air before a midwest electrical storm; charged with ions and pungent with ozone. But it wasn't only the air that sizzled, the consonants did, too. And the rhythms crackled with energy.

None of us is Shaw or Hirt, least of all me. We can't all be brilliant, possessed and magically leonine. In Hirt's case, impossibly handsome to boot. Lucy Hirt, Charles' widow, said to me after a recent Chamber Choir performance at USC, "You're not as good as Charles yet, honey, but you're getting there." No, I'm not, Lucy, and thanks, but I doubt I'll ever get there. Despite being Just Plain Bill, however, here's what I've managed to surmise about the reason that handsome pair, Rhythm and Pitch, are on the social A-list and appear at all the fashionable parties.

Dehning's Deduction

Rhythm makes people think. Pitch makes them groan. Rhythm is a comely, witty wench all by herself, fun to be with. Without Rhythm by his side, Pitch is a didactic, demanding dullard. I'll refine that first sentence: rhythm makes people think *ahead.* And *not thinking ahead is the major cause of poor intonation and pitch.* Which takes us right back to the beginning of this topic: Brain, Body, Breath. I've punished myself silly a zillion times searching through the small catalogue of causes and solutions I've written above, trying to help the ensemble through a thicket of pitch or intonation when all I really needed to do was stop and calmly say "think." It often works.

Here is the primary rehearsal exhortation I have uttered thousands of times throughout my entire career:

- "We don't care what kind of sound you sing, or what pitch you sing it on, but we want it on time, every time."
- "Sing something on the right beat, we don't care what."
- "Be on time with the money."

And so on, in countless variations. This tends to alleviate another musical phenomenon detrimental to intonation that seems unique to choral music: following. Brie waits for Suzie to sing the pitch and then comes in. Brie not only comes in late, she comes in flat, invariably, because she's following. Brie needs to take a few risks and think for herself. She needs to be on time with the money, instead of trying to pick up somebody else's paycheck. Maybe she would gain some skill in musicianship, thereby giving herself the self-esteem she so craves. More cheaply than by visiting a therapist, too. "She can plant her own garden," my Minnesota aunts and uncles would have said. (Hence the expression "tough row to hoe." Some rows are hard, some easy. Hoeing rows is hard, backbreaking work, though. I don't think there was ever any row I hoed as a boy that wasn't tough. And Viking descendants don't cheer "good job!" when you've finished your row, tough or not. They grunt – if that – and direct you to several more.)

I heard John Alldis say that "it's sometimes amazing how quickly the notes come if you go after the music." I agree, and I will amend that by backing up in the process a bit and saying that I find it amazing how quickly the pitches come if we go after the rhythm. In the beginning of the rehearsal process, my priorities are, in rough order: style, rhythm, text, vocal sound, pitch, balance, dynamic. First thing we gotta do is say something well. Then we gotta say it together.

Precision

"In the beginning was rhythm," Hans von Bülow said. One of his countrymen, Wilhelm Ehmann, said this about half a century later:

"Rhythm is the binding, governing principle in music. Rhythm is a stronger factor than sheer sound in unifying individual singers into a choral unit. At the point where rhythm is caught and mastered, the musician experiences a kind of abandonment to the music."

About the time Ehmann was writing his book, I was listening to an American Francophile with a German surname (Hirt) say this, "There's a misconception regarding precision; that it is simply starting and stopping together. No, it is mainly an *organic movement through an entire line*. This is not a mechanical or intellectual thing, it is an inner concept."

What the American with a German surname (Dehning) writing this book has to say about rhythm and precision is nowhere near as profound. It is an attempt to make statements like the above a bit more accessible to us mortals by filling in some of the spaces between the words with concepts. (I read somewhere recently that real poetry is in the spaces between words. I like the concept. I'm a concept kind of guy – have I said that?)

Rhythm

The first concept is Pulse. Here's a vocabulary of rhythm: meter, tempo, pulse. The greatest of these is pulse (some call it "beat," but I use that word for other things. Besides, pulse is physically correct). Meter is mere organization of pulse into "measures" of varying amounts. Tempo is merely rate of pulse. Pulse, in contrast, is as holy as my heartbeat. Nothing "mere" about it. It is the carpet upon which rhythm reclines.

Most of us were taught to "count" rhythms in the early stages of our musical training: "one-two-and-three-four," or: "three-ee-and-a-four-

and." Such procedures make us do the math, which in the beginning is probably necessary. One problem with it, though, is that you can get the speech part right and still get the rhythm part wrong, as I used to do as a boy in lessons (with the proudest, cutest smile). This is because counting is a logical procedure. Singing and playing, however, are not logical procedures. They are aesthetic and physical phenomena. We are concerned with a unity of *being*, especially in ensemble.

Pulsing Away

I see "counting-glyphs" on scores that are passed in all the time: such diligence, such thoroughness, worthy of praise. Such a waste of time, worthy of tears. In complicated rhythmic passages, with sixteenth notes flying everywhere, in all combinations, full of meter changes, ties, dots, and what-have-you, I ask – no require – that the ensemble use a pencil and make a vertical slash on the beginning of every *pulse*. That's all they need to do, that's their job and it takes a nanosecond. Then the Shaw Technique of Counting[1] can work, too. This consists of counting smallest rhythmic denominators (one-and-two-and-three-and-four-and) practically all of the time at the beginning of the learning process, and resorting to it many times thereafter. (I don't use this much, by the way, but only in the most difficult of rhythmic passages. I have it in my arsenal of teaching techniques, is all. I don't have his capacity to do it constantly, and with every piece, without driving the ensemble straight to the Ha-Ha Hotel. Maybe because I'm not Shaw.) If they want to know how many pulses are in the measure or how fast the pulses go at the moment, they've got me for that: that's my job, else what good am I? When their scores are passed in, I want to see *slashes* all over them, not numbers!

My own scores – especially full scores and all recitatives – were slashed to bits before theirs were ever passed out. I need to have straight in my head not only what's what, but who's where and, most important, WHEN. I make sure I hear this in dense rhythmic textures by having them sing every note short on "pah" or some such, not holding any note longer than the smallest common denominator. This exercise does two things: it allows *me* to hear the inner rhythm of each pulse and makes *them* think –

---

1 *One - ee - and - a, two - ee - and - a*

they can't "follow" because they only get one whack at the note.

Phrasing Away

While they are slashing their way through scores, I've been doing something insidious and sneaky: I've been **working in *phrases*** 90% of the time, only stopping for the first-aid of working on a beat or two with seriously wounded rhythms. I want them to quickly grasp a rhythmic entity – a line – which "allows them to perform freely and confidently." (I think I got that from Ehmann. Look it up, would you?) This is essentially what Hirt called "organic movement through the line."   And unless these phrases have been melismatic, I've kept the text in as we repeat, because most of the time the rhythms are based on text, as are the phrases, as is *musical* articulation. By teaching the ensemble to quickly absorb a phrase or line, I'm hoping they will learn to master larger musical relationships, be less stuck in the score and avoid singing one note at a time. All "*good* things," as Brie would say, upward inflection and smile on the first word.

As to sound, I've concentrated so far on the vowels alone, because – all together now – the sound is the vowel.

Meanwhile, I've begun to remind them to *breathe* for this whole phrase and to breathe soon enough, because breathing takes time, as I recall. John Alldis often said in rehearsal, sometimes even with his pros, "You're breathing when you should be singing." I say it often, too, or something similar. Breath is rhythm.

Beginning to Show Off

The eye sees a space on the page between words that exists neither in song nor in speech; in reality, in other words. "We . .don't . .talk . . like . .this." Bush II does, I know, which is why I'd rather read what he said the next day. I can't take it Live From the White House. I keep holding my breath and nodding off from asphyxia waiting for the comma or period. Like awaiting the second verb in German. Listening to a lecture in German is an exercise in suspense. Mark Twain said that "one could, the entire history of the Thirty Years War between verbs put." Funny, bright man. We don't sing like that either, instead incorporating a principle derived from the French word *liaison*.

That word means "go between," roughly. In song, consonants go between the vowels. I talked about this principle in regard to diction but it also has enormous implications for precision. Here's how it works.

What we see is: his eye is on the sparrow;

What we sing is: h[I]-z[ɑ]-[I]z[ɔ]n-th[ɑ]-sp[æ]-r[o]

Put into words, any last consonant of a word or syllable becomes the first consonant of the next word or syllable (true of the vanishing vowel in a diphthong, too: the little thing just moves right on over). This is how we should sing most Indo-European languages, with the exception of German. If we apply this principle most of the time – almost make an axiom of it – we'll not only get a terrific vocal *legato*, we'll begin to get rhythms that snap-crackle-pop, and ensemble precision that glistens. ("Glisten" reminds me of *Karate Kid* and waxing my Righteous Red Rocket. There is no such thing as a "one simple step" car cleaner-polish-wax that really does the job. To do it right, you have to go through three separate processes: first the cleaner, then the polish, then the wax. No short cuts. No easy way out.) Consonant liaison is the wax, the last thing we do, supplying the *internal* consonants to the line. I need to go back to the beginning again and talk about some agents present in the cleaner we're using.

Cleaning Agents

The second eighth note, the last pulse in a bar, the last three of four sixteenths. We must love all of these children, not just the ones at the beginning of the pulse, the ones born first (right, Meggie?). Listen for them from the beginning and listen for them to the end. Ensembles tend to take them for granted and not give them their place in time, their due duration, mainly. "Little notes have a right to life, too," Shaw said. "Sing like Jimmy Cagney," Dehning says ("you-u di-i-r-ty-y ra-at,"with equal stress on all syllables).

Ties and dots: if slow and *legato*, I ask for almost a *crescendo* through these, fattening the vowel and using liaison lavishly, wax-to-the-max. If fast and *legato*, or with any other combination of tempo and articulation at all, we don't need these ties and dots. Do what a good marching band does. Sometimes emphasize the note after the tie or dot, as a good jazz band does. "Get off those ties, throw away those dots," I say. "Who needs, 'em?" Salamunovich asks.

Rests. "Rests don't mean 'repose,'" Hirt said, amplifying, "the lights don't go out at a quarter rest." "Unless you're breathing, don't 'fall into' those rests," Salamunovich says. Swan said, finger wagging furiously, "A rest does one of two things: it either gathers or dissipates energy." "Use rests as tools," I implore. "If dissipating energy, use it for a full breath. If gathering energy, think through it, use it as a springboard into the next phrase, a la the latest short female gymnast," I say. (That Dehning! Him and his "tools!")

And now, I say, time for me to shower, trim the beard, walk the *Paseo Maritimo*, eat the midday meal, take a siesta, get on to the next chapter.

THE ENSEMBLE: SISTERS

I'm back. (I'll work until 9:00, then it'll be time for tapas – *"pintxos"* here in Spanish Basqueland – book, and bed. Then I'm going to take a break and buzz around French Basqueland for a few days; do some shopping for My Women in a language I can handle better, even though the French don't think so. You know, last night after *pintxos* I was paying the bartender and he asked, "Deutsch?," deducing from genes and jeans, I guess, that is what I must be. I tower above most of these strong little buggers, and still wear jeans with *elán*. I responded, "No, *Senor, norteamericano.*" The inference I drew from his reaction to my response was, "This guy is here in *October*, speaking the language – at least *trying* – and he's an *American?!*" Naturally, Leo that I am, I puffed up on the spot with both pride and accomplishment; went to bed more content than usual. Male ego is really something, isn't it?)

The sisters in choral sound are **balance and dynamic**. These two are at least psychically, if not always physically, inseparable. Balance is relative to dynamic. Many people still confuse balance with blend, as I said, and confuse blend with dynamic, too, if you want to know the truth. Let's forget blend entirely for the moment, or forever, if you like.   The Sisters are concerned primarily with representing the composer's intentions as present in the score; to make certain that even though a score may show a *tutti mf*, the thematic elements in that framework are a little more than *mf*, or that others are a little less. The Sisters will have it no other way. They are the composer's advocate at all times.

The Numbers Game

I have said (actually, Hirt said it. I stole it. He didn't mind. You want it? It's yours. I don't mind). that balance is the "equalization of the quantity of tone within and between sections." Geometrically, this would look like a square, with sopranos on top and basses on the bottom (tenor and alto in the middle where they belong). You could say that's ideal or you could disagree; depends on concept, as does everything. I disagree a little bit. In most situations, I'd like the basses to be a little more than equal, I like a slightly bottom-heavy sound, with the bottom of that square extended a bit on both sides. Roger Wagner and then through him, Paul Salamunovich like(d) a very bottom heavy sound coupled with a *very* light soprano sound. This gives a shape more like an isosceles triangle, again with sopranos on top.

We should try to accomplish our concept of balance in terms of numbers first, realizing that if the voices are younger, the lower ones (alto and bass) do not have the vocal authority of the upper. We don't want these lower voices to force the tone for reasons of both vocal health and intonation so we might want to numerically overload the lower sections a bit if possible. So instead of four per part in a chamber choir, we could have 4-5-4-5, reading from higher voices to lower; in larger groups of the same age, 12-14-9-14. I have found such geometry and arithmetic to work together quite well.

Bad-Geometry Problems with Some Solutions

Why only nine tenors in that last example? Probably because I couldn't find any more. What most of us get geometrically in a lot of situations is a triangle standing on its tip, not its base, with tenors at the tip and sopranos still on top. Bad news.

And these sopranos are oftentimes not all youthful, dewy-eyed, fluffy little things with smarts, like Suzie. If young and ambitious, out to "make her bones," (as they might say in the Italian Club) she is determined to prove her worth and beauty with volume alone, to heck with smarts. Her name is Victoria, and she is flinty-eyed. To her *mf* means mighty forte, *mp* means mucho plenty, and *ff* is fully frightening, often fortified with tremolo (not vibrato). *Pianissimo* is not in her arsenal and I do mean arsenal – the voice is often used as a weapon, against sister sopranos to begin with, the rest of the world thereafter. And she will prevail, she will prevail. If no longer so young or ambitious, if in fact reaching my age and older, evolving from Victoria to Cruella, the above sound is just as loud but becomes thinner, and the tremolo has metastasized into a wobble (not vibrato) that spans a minor third, on occasion achieving the tri-tone. So help me God. No! wait! no, I am not kidding, I am not exaggerating. I have lived through all this. I am not exaggerating. We generally forget the unpleasant things with time, thank heaven. Not so with these two.

They are with me still, and will be until I cross over into campground, at which point I hope to watch them disappear downstream. No hyperbole. I am not kidding.

All is not lost. Forsaking homicide for the moment, there are a number of things we can do with our inverted triangle, even with Victoria. (I can't talk about Cruella anymore.) To begin with, we should audition all of these voices at least annually, in the sense of "audir = to hear." Listen to them one-on-one, paying especially close attention to the weight of the voice and to where it breaks, with an ear toward voices that could help the tenor and alto lines now and then for short periods of time. We're looking for "switch hitters," people who can bat both left and right; reinforcements to rush to the front if a hole develops in the line. If the baritone is light, he can help the tenor in the lower tessitura. If the alto has some weight, she can help the tenor in the very high tessitura. If the soprano has some weight and a good bottom, she can help the alto. If the soprano's bottom is very full and free, beg her to sing alto most or much of the time. (Victoria sings second soprano, not first. If she gives you any lip about it, tell her to report to Sergeant Park in the alto squad immediately, and to remain there. Sergeant Park will set her straight. She has a black belt in *hapkiddo* and relishes the opportunity to strap it on.)

Once we can get the sopranos straightened out we need to realize that, in terms of numbers, we can get by with fewer men than women and still approach some kind of balanced sound because the men's voices are heavier. We can survive. We also need to keep in mind that, with a few adjustments, it is easier for the voice to sing higher than normal, as opposed to lower than normal. Thus, in an exposed tenor line in mid-voice, I've thrown all the basses into the breach countless times if volume is called for. And though volume and sonority are not the same thing, the latter will do in a pinch. "Safety in numbers" and all that. The same is true with sopranos helping out an exposed alto line.

Musical Chairs (sorry)

I said before that seating arrangement can affect intonation. True. But it affects balance more and for the same reason: people in the ensemble may hear better, listen more readily. What we want in terms of balance is for the listeners in the *audience* to hear better what the composer may have had in mind. I'm not going to go into the zillions of formations. The trick in seating formation of any kind is to try to ensure that the switch hitters are near both sections they have to help. Hirt called it "voice phasing." This might be the ideal formation for this purpose:

B2-B1-T2-T1
S1-S2-A1-A2

Now singers can move easily from one voice part to another. This also has the advantage of the acoustical connection of outer voices – basses and sopranos – who often have octaves that must be in tune. It may be the ideal for any purpose. This is my standard, point-and-shoot formation.

Below is the European form of this, the one I often use with orchestra because vocal and instrumental basses can come from the same side of the stage:

T1-T2-B1-B2
S1-S2-A1-A2

It would be nice to use one of these all the time but numbers don't always allow it. Back to that inverted triangle. I omit 1st and 2nd considerations from here on, because such niceties are less important in these situations. I will say that, except for the B2, I tend to put 2nds near the front. I've used this, men-in-the-middle:

SSBBA
STAA

. . .And its sibling:

SSTAA
SBBA

. . .with decent results, involving ratios (women/men) of 7/4, even 2/1, maybe even 3/1. Beyond 3/1, balance hasn't a chance. Consider going into administration or coaching (same thing).

What the last two do is bring the male sound forward. The next one does too, and is another I may use with orchestra for the same reason as the "Euro" one or in just another attempt to hear the men, to give them a chance:

SSATB

SAATB

With smaller choirs (40 and under), the following will accomplish that same purpose, maybe better. I've used it very often:

SSBSSBAATAA

SSBSSBAATAA

Even if numerical balance is ideal and I want a blast of Brut® now and then, I have found this very effective:

SBSBATAT

SBSBATAT

Omelet by Attribute

Numbers are not the only consideration in seating, however. There are three more that I take into consideration: size of voice, acuity of ear, timbre of voice.   The latter is similar to Father William Finn's categorization of voices into instrumental qualities; flute, violin, etc. For instance, I like a mix of violas and horns in the tenor section, trombones and cellos in the basses (tubas are hard to find).

Back to size.   It's generally not a good idea to put all *stronger* (S) voices of the same voice part together, and all *lighter* (L) voices of the same voice part together, like this:

SSSLLLL

I think the following is better because the strong are more likely to listen to the light, possibly aiding balance. I say "possibly," because I'm not altogether convinced that the meek inherit the earth in such situations:

LSLSLSL

Now to *ear* (E). The same consideration can apply in terms of aural acuity. Some singers have very fine musicianship, others are still learning. Some have fine, natural *voices* (V); others have a ways to go via training. I do the same as with L/S:

EVEVEVE

In the last two formations, I have placed light voices and singers with good musicianship to the outside because I want them to influence the others, to sing inward toward the others, but also for another reason. Maybe others have found otherwise, but I have found that in general the better musicians have lighter voices, while the stronger voices often lack musical confidence and tend not to be the best of sight readers. Naturally, exceptions exist and we encounter a singer with perfect pitch, a fine big voice, and a sense of taste and propriety. These are not found around every corner, at least in this life.

Years ago, I kept moving Cheryl farther and farther toward the outside because, despite a quite powerful voice, I could never hear much of her in rehearsal. For months. You know the end of this story: at the performance we had a figurative cannon booming from our left flank, overwhelming the small arms fire emanating from all around her. She had finally learned the music from all the Karens and Suzies in her squad and she was now firing proudly at will. Balance for the whole ensemble went into the tank. For me, another lesson learned the hard way. (Want another? Never put two Victorias within firing range of one another. Keep them as far apart as possible. They will either love to sing together, which is bad, or they will hate to sing together, which is worse. One of them will not emerge alive and ensemble balance will have been laid waste, the victim of a prolonged competitive siege.)

Front Lines and Reinforcements

We need voices like Cheryl's violin, though, because a soprano section of flutes alone lacks color and power, at least for me. But the trick is, we need at least two of them. One will not do, because of balance. In a section of six, I like two violins, one oboe, one muted trumpet, two flutes. (Altos, by the way, are clarinets, violas and horns – both French and English – in just about any combination.)

And the reason I kept moving Cheryl to the outside years ago is that I tend to group stronger voices – double reeds and brass – toward the center and back of the ensemble, surrounding them with lighter voices - strings and flutes, somewhat like so:

LSSSSL
LLSSSL
LLSSLL
LLSLLL

I find that the foregoing arrangement tends to lend a center core to the choral sound, much like focus in the individual voice surrounded by the ambient halo of warmer, lighter colors and overtones.

And yes, I'm aware of Weston Noble's method of sectional seating, but it takes more time than I am willing to expend, given the return. It does work. In a way, I do use it but in telescoped form, by moving individual singers around from time to time over the course of a semester or a year. The point I want to make here is that we must experiment with seating constantly, based on what we're hearing from the voices and how a given piece is sounding. No two groups are the same any more than any two people are, and what works well one year may come to naught the next. But we must start somewhere and we must arrive somewhere, finally – at least two weeks before a performance, incidentally – so that the singers become accustomed to what they are hearing around them.

One principle to which I adhere at almost any cost is that the singers need room to operate and breathe; the voice needs room to sound. A distance of three feet from shoulder to shoulder and from row to row is ideal, but not always possible. If I cannot give them room front to back, I at least make certain that they have decent lateral room. When in doubt, add more risers or more rows or something, if only for acoustical reasons. I have noticed on many previous occasions that our little forty-voice ensemble from University of the Pacific (UOP), spread comfortably over the entire eight risers at collegiate festivals, sounded louder than choruses twice our size that were crammed up there bellybuttons to bummies. In short, the voice operates best not only with space inside, but *outside* it, too.

Keeping Score

Many balance problems are inherent in the music itself, long before we bring our ensemble to it, balanced or not. I do not hesitate to re-voice a score for purposes of balance, sometimes ease, if I honestly feel that I can represent the composer's score better by doing it. For instance, in the common *divisi*, SSA, does the composer really mean divide sopranos and leave altos intact? So if we have 6S and 6A, should it be 3-3-6? Is the same true of SAA, yielding 6-3-3? Sometimes the *divisi* is clearly indicated by a bracket on either S or A, but more often than not we're left with our own decisions regarding the purpose of the *divisi* and what implications it has for balance. When SSA is indicated, I assume that composers want each voice sounded equally, so I usually voice it 4-4-4. If I see SAA, I invariably use 4-4-4, and if the alto tessitura lies particularly low, 4-3-5. It often means that those switch hitters need a road map to figure out where they go but the final results are very balanced to my ear.

Speaking of switch hitters, if the music is fugal or highly imitative, a device of balance I learned from Roger Wagner back in the early sixties is to have those people sing nothing but entries for long stretches of the piece. They'll sing the soprano subject almost to completion and then jump down and sing the same subject with the altos. And so on. Wagner's reason for doing this was that he wanted the *audience* to hear what the composer wrote, so he gave Bach a hand in modern times with modern instruments, and women's voices rather than boys. It works.

So does something else I learned from Wagner in those years, but learned later that it came from Shaw. If the group was large – 32 voices or more – Shaw assigned a certain minority in each section to sing all fast melismatic passages *staccato*, which cleans up the line considerably. I worked on this idea for a while, then came up with my own perversion of it. If there are six per part, I will ask two of them to insert a consonant – usually [n] using only the tip of the tongue – before whichever vowel is being sung in the melisma at the time. It *sounds staccato* to the audience because of the consonant, but the singer isn't actually singing *staccato*. Not bad for a dumb Norseman, eh? It really works nicely. After a performance of Bach's *Singet* with the California Choral Company in Phoenix, Beth Avakian came running up breathlessly:

— "How did you *do* that?! How did you perform it at that tempo so *cleanly?*"
— "We cheated," I said, and told her.
— This time it was someone else's turn to say, "Oh."

Scrambled or Sunny-side Up

It is approaching fetish. It is long past trend, fad, or fashion for many ensembles to sing everything "scrambled," or mixed into quartets. It has become a badge of honor and pride and accomplishment in many circles, occasionally involving sneers of derision and taunts of incompetence toward ensembles that don't do so. There is a reason that professional ensembles with extensive repertoire, or symphony choruses that work often with orchestra, don't use this formation, and it's a simple one.

You can't conduct them in performance.

No, don't give me that, I'm not listening. There's no way you can *clearly, without confusion* on someone's part ("Who? Me? Him? Them? Us?") ask the altos for a little more sound, or prepare the sopranos for a tricky entrance, or help remind the basses to shape a consistently troublesome vowel correctly. Nor can a tenor section spread from Kuala Lumpur to Vladivostok be in tune with itself. "No way, Jose," as my wife says in her elegant Spanish.

Singing in quartets has a number of beneficial effects on the ensemble and individual singers that I have already mentioned, but I'll repeat them here to make a point. Because the singers hear all parts, this formation can enhance balance, intonation and blend in a short time. And singers love it because they hear both themselves and others around them equally well. It's fun. So I use this formation in music which calls for such attributes, that is, homophonic, softer pieces with sexy harmonies, especially "vocal jazz" arrangements of ballads; also in some Romantic part-songs and secular Renaissance pieces where I might want to ask just a quartet or two to sing a verse for dynamic, textural variety. That's it. And that's about 20% of our repertoire. The rest of the time we perform in sections.

Doing What It Does Best

I said "perform." With a new group at the beginning of the year, I usually seat them in quartets, often spread out a bit. This doesn't simply enhance musical independence, it enforces it. We rehearse that way for quite a while, until it has become apparent to all of us that the individual singers know what they are doing. And we know who doesn't, as do they, quite often – unless they're tenors, and this is important information for everyone, including those tenors. I even use this formation in the first call-back audition when ensemble personnel is not yet final and everyone is sight-reading. Talk about posture! Those quadriceps are flexed and those gluteus maximi are one centimeter off the chair and the gears in those brains are turning so fast you can see smoke coming out their ears. These people are paying a-t-t-e-n-t-i-o-n!

Are they watching me that closely? Heck, no. Do I care? (Same answer.) I'm using my ears and my eyes, not my arms. The latter are for later. I don't conduct them until they're ready. If I insisted on it too early, it would only frustrate us all. At this stage, I am teacher and coach. Midway to the performance, I come up with a sectional plan and we use it from then on out. I ask them to watch me increasingly more, giving me my role in the music making process which is to help them perform in a manner satisfying and enjoyable to all, but most important to the singer. And, boy, do I conduct them then.

I don't know anyone else who uses this strategy. If you, yourself, do, would you contact me and let me know, especially if you find it as effective as I do? Maybe we're both just weird.

Dynamic

With the possible exception of intonation – and even there, several strong cases could be made – every aspect of choral sound under discussion thus far is relative to many factors, most of those factors involving people, whether performer or audience. Dynamic is the most relative of them all, partaking far less of mathematics and the sciences than the others. Like balance, it has to do with quantity of sound. But also, like diction and blend, it has to do with quality of sound. There is almost no technique in dynamic; it is entirely concept, poetry. Maybe even philosophy. It is the most subjective of all the parameters of music.

There's a misconception regarding dynamic, which is that it deals only in volume, in amplitude and decibels. That's extrinsic. More important to us, dynamic also involves incentive, which is intrinsic. Robert Stevenson wrote a dissertation on the relationship of intensity and dynamic a long, long time ago at UCLA You could look it up. I just looked up incentive in the thesaurus myself. Synonyms are motive, inspiration, stimulus. At its most elemental level, though, incentive means "reason," and that reason lies in emotional content. So follow me now, because here it is and it's short.

Dynamic comes from intensity, which comes from incentive, which comes from emotional content. Put the other way around:

Emotion yields incentive yields intensity + (amplitude to taste) = dynamic.

And there we have it.

To illustrate this link between emotion and incentive, a high Bb, or a strong, good sound of any kind, comes easier with fear. If you see a man about to step off a curb in front of a quickly approaching car, your resultant yell of warning (HEY!!) will be *marcato*, well supported and fully resonated. The body coordinated because it knew what it wanted to say. Read that last sentence again, even though you've seen variations of it before. A marine drill sergeant and a cheerleader get hoarse because they are trying to *instill* the emotion; fear in the first case, enthusiasm in the second. Our ensembles, regardless of age, will sing maturely and with a full range of dynamic and not get tired if incentive is present. We must give them a reason for doing what they're doing. "Reason" may be the wrong word, implying logical motive and Greek philosophical processes, but it's all I have. The word I'm looking for lies somewhere deep down in the primordial ooze from whence we sprang, in the well-spring of our very being. I don't know what that word is. Here's how we can dance around it:

Imagery

— "Take a loud tone and compress it" (for *pp*)
— "Make it shimmer"
— "Sing as loudly as you can softly"
— "Don't just whisper the *pp*, whisper the *ff*, too"

— "Sing through the eyes. All the time. Loud or soft"
— "You sing *fortes* angry all the time. Try the right emotion: joy, fear, love, desolation, madness, delirium. You know what's right as well as I do" (and they do).

Sources of Incentive

That last one is critical. Every dynamic in the well-written piece was put there for a reason, in an attempt to evoke a quality of sound which expresses an emotion, which is probably present in the text and it isn't always stereotyped. *Pianissimo* can rejoice; *fortissimo* can lament.

The most powerful suggestive source for the ensemble in terms of dynamic quality is not words, though. It is us. The conductor. We must take on the emotional and physical characteristics of the music. Not just "be the music," be *inside* the music. We must express a quality of dynamic with our whole being. If we do, the group will respond empathetically. Unlike sympathy, empathy is a two-way avenue (rapport of any kind is simply an extreme form of empathy). Being "inside the music" is the surest cure for self-consciousness on our part that I know of. In rehearsal, I don't know if I'm perceived as cute or cool or profound or dumb or weird. I'm too far away for that. I'm on another planet. I could be working at the University of Pluto for all I know. More important, for all I care. What matters is that the ensemble knows (no, *senses*) that all I do care about is getting that music off the page and into our souls for just a moment. What we want is for the taught to take on the goals and purposes of the teacher, who only wants the message to come through.

Then, and only then, are we home.

Byproduct I: Second Person Singular For Once

I've been relating a lot of methods and opinions about choral sound, most of them my own. Just for some perspective, I thought a number of you might want to get even a bit or read someone *else's* opinion about my work, in case you don't have one of your own, or in case you do, and don't like it (my work, not your opinion). That's fair. Especially since this doesn't come with a CD or a video. Here you go, then.

In June, 2000, Amy Stuart Hunn finished a master's thesis at Stanford University with the title, *Choral Sonority: A Comparative Analysis of Seven Choral Tone Paradigms*. The paradigms included, in addition to mine, were Charlene Archibeque, Anton Armstrong, Vance George, Craig Jessop, Paul Salamunovich, and Dale Warland. I was surprised and flattered to get the call and do the interview. Truly. That's pretty good company, I'd say. Mrs. Hunn not only made some fine observations – sometimes delicately phrased, given the firepower in her lineup (present company excluded). She is also a superb writer and an obviously intelligent woman. It is Stanford, after all. And she's quite objective.

I mailed the only (tsk, tsk) CD we've made in my years at USC, which was compiled from DATs made in one take from 1994 to 1997, predominantly the latter (it was a great year). The chorus numbered 20-24 (primarily the latter). Here are most of the references she made to me and my work in the forty-one pages of her thesis. No editing for ego, though. "Good" and "bad" are all here.

— While Dehning and Armstrong agree in principle on [working with student ensembles], their choirs are as qualitatively different as any two ensembles in this study. Dehning's choir may not attain the full power of a professional ensemble, but the voices in the group are certainly much larger than those in the St. Olaf Choir. The [USC voice faculty] must appreciate Dehning's approach to choral tone and a more soloistic vocal technique than that advocated by Armstrong.

— [Salamunovich] makes for an interesting contrast to William Dehning; both work with operatic voices, but Dehning allows those voices to sing with, in his words, the "free voice," while Salamunovich extracts a wider range of expression and tonal quality through greater control of the voice.

— In Archibeque's paradigm, vocal pedagogy is a tool for realizing an aesthetic aim; for Armstrong and Dehning, pedagogy and aesthetic are virtually one and the same. [Bulls-eye, Mrs. Hunn. – author]

— Opinions differed, however, on the question of the ideal range of vibrato acceptable in a choral ensemble. The fact that William Dehning describes the North-Central European choral sound as "really quite a straight sound" demonstrates this. . .Clearly, Armstrong and Dehning have different concepts of what straight tone *is*. A cursory review of their respective choral recordings strongly suggests that they have quite different

concepts of what "full tone" is, as well.
— The very same "student model," when applied by William Dehning, produces a very different result. . .his choral paradigm favors richness, color and power to a greater degree than Armstrong's does. Like Armstrong, he exploits the strengths of the voices in his ensemble; unlike Armstrong, those voices happen to be larger, more operatic ones.
— [Dehning] is not as enthusiastic [about European choral sound], but acknowledges their influence on his work. However, he later mentions the sixteen-voice professional English ensemble, the John Alldis Choir, with more gusto: ". . .sixteen professional singers who could really *sing*. It was tremendous . . ." (Although English, it should be noted that the John Alldis Choir does not sing with anything approaching the stereotypical English choral tone. Rather, its tone quality is close to that of an ensemble of soloists.)
— In the [USC] Choir, the colorful mosaic of tone can mask technical flaws in the individual voices; different colors and timbres gain prominence at different times, but this is consistent with Dehning's fundamental aesthetic. . .As I have already mentioned, the [USC] Choir demonstrates the least tonal homogeneity of any of the surveyed ensembles.

So now, if nothing else, you know how heterogeneous our sound is perceived to be – maybe, in fact, is. I'm too close to it to know, which is why I included the foregoing. Most of that CD was from 96-97, as I said, and the six altos that year included one Jordanian, two Koreans, one Hungarian, one Bulgarian, and one Caucasian. Talk about heterogeneous! Their section skit on tour was getting into as much native garb as possible and then holding a mock sectional in which they each spoke their native languages simultaneously. "Funny" doesn't begin to describe the result. They won the Conductor's Award for Best Skit. I'm really not sure what we might have done to get a homogeneous sound out of that bunch that year, short of gene replacement.

Byproduct II: Back to First Person Singular

I don't know how I did it, I certainly didn't plan it, but this last chapter about choral sound has evolved smoothly into the topic of performance. I say "evolve" also because the original outline had a chapter following the next one entitled The Product, which was to be about performance. I viewed performance as the natural culmination of chapters 2-8, which I suppose it is. Some might say that we would then have arrived at the Apex, the Zenith, the Goal, the Purpose of the previous chapters. Maybe those people are right. I guess. I mean, the date of the performance is in the calendar, isn't it? Been there a long time, since long before that first rehearsal. We've been "slouching toward Bethlehem" and now here we are. Why am I not on my knees in wonder? Why am I not jittery with anticipation like I was before ball games? Why am I not rubbing my hands with glee, exhorting knights to the ramparts, damsels to the castle keep?

I just can't go into it here: flowers for the girls, boot-in-the-rears for the boys? How to get on and off stage? Houselights up or down? Program format and content? Chorus turn pages with the soloists? Sound checks? Order of stage bows? Milk or not? Perfume or not? Fainting on stage? (Debbie Helmholtz took out the entire tenor section once. If I'd used scattered formation, tenor casualties might have been fewer.) How to give pitches? Smile or not? How much/what kind of warm-up? Folders or not, right hand or left hand, when up, when down? How high the heels? "How High the Moon?" And so on.

Why can't choruses just amble out there like orchestras do, stand around, hum and buzz a bit, do some plumbing, suck on some reeds, fine tune the pantyhose, bow ties and a few chords, sing a few licks, take a cue from lobby lights – oops, conductor walking out – and here we go? (I actually tried this once just for the heck of it, to post-concert yelps of indignation from the audience and the reviewer. Hee-hee. You believe that? Yeah, you believe it.)

I will say one thing about all this, but a lot of you aren't going to like it. Can we American choruses please do away with those ensemble bows from the waist? They represent false humility on the part of the conductor, for one thing. They are never together, for another. How can they be? We are not theatre troupes (they are small), dancers (they are few) or marching bands (they are quasi-military fanatics). My high school marching band bowed better than all you guys, not because I was their drum major but because we spent a lot of time drilling all that stuff. You want to spend a bunch of your precious rehearsal time getting it together? Let's say you do. What does the audience (this *is* stagecraft, after all) get from your drilled unison movement? Instead of a mutant, many-tentacled sea anemone in twelve feet of water waving slowly toward them, they get this sudden lurch of a monster cut in half and then magically restored to wholeness. The larger the group, the worse the effect. No matter how accomplished, the surfeit of movement doth incite my innards to rebellion; in sooth, doth make my stomach heave.

And while I'm at it. Can we go back to "chorus" or "choir"? Dispense with the "chorale" stuff? Especially *Master* Chorale? How many "masters" can there be, given the Bell Curve and all? Let the L.A. Master Chorale have it, since it was Roger Wagner's idea back in 1967, I think. As to "chorale," let it revert to either a French adjective or a Lutheran hymn tune or both. Let's can the glam. And I keep seeing "Chamber" Singers the size of Roman regiments. All of this stuff devalues the currency. What's in a name? Plenty.

Some trendoids say that "god" is in the details. For me, there be demons lurking in them (I *hate* messing with dresses for the women. Hate it. Hate it. Hate. *It.* That and committees are the Purgatory of my Position). I don't mean to trivialize such things, because they do matter. They just drive me nuts and I do my best to be aware of them and then to beg someone else to keep an eye on them for me. Please. I can't keep too many balls in the air at once: I start dropping some. I worked for banks for a couple of years and rarely balanced to double zero at the end of the day. But when the lobby got crowded, and the Operations Manager yelled, "Dehning, get on that teller line," the addition of my window alone cleared that lobby in minutes. Double zeros weren't that important to me, empty lobbies were. Still are.

Some witty, wise wag once said that life is what happens to us when we're not looking. Performance is what happens to me when I show up at a rehearsal one day, have someone else conduct for a while, take a step back, and look and listen: yep, sounds like a chorus, smells like one, looks like one, too, by golly. Guess we're ready to run this flag up the pole and see if anyone salutes.

Performance is dessert and coffee – rehearsal is appetizer and main course.

My daughter, Megan, says, "Beer has food value. Food doesn't have beer value."

That's My Girl!

For more such wisdom, dear reader, read on, read on. . .

THE PROCESS

The Longest Introductory Exposition in the Book

This may be yet another example of my weirdness, but I enjoy rehearsals more than performances. I love to rehearse. No, I *live* to rehearse. Especially at that point when the notes are not quite there yet, but the ensemble has grasped the framework of the piece or pieces, and understands why we are beginning to work on communicating its essence. Like on weekend retreats in the fall, or day-long "attacks" on Washington's birthday, or, no, hey, better yet, that first rehearsal with chorus and orchestra, where the chorus is ready and the orchestra is oblivious and I watch their ears and eyes come open. Man! That is living! Taking all those wildly alien elements of a perplexity and hammering them together? For me, "getting there" is almost all the fun.

Don't get me wrong. Performances are fun, too, but they are not creative like rehearsals are: they are more re-creative for me. I sweat a lot more in performance than in rehearsal because I am concerned more for the ensemble than for myself. My job is finished. Now it's their turn and I want them to enjoy it as much as humanly possible. I want to help them do so and I don't want to do anything to screw it up for them, so I really sweat. Even so, I manage to give the impression that I know what I'm doing. After an ACDA performance with the Chamber Choir in Pasadena (CA, not TX), Sherrie Paine, Gordon's wife, got into the same elevator with me:

— "Bill, that was wonderful."
— "Thanks, Sherrie, that means a lot, coming from you."
— "You were born to do that."
— "Oh. Gosh. Well." (That Dehning is always so articulate!)

As I said earlier in this book, efficient and enjoyable rehearsing is one of my three strengths, according to outside opinions I respect. I still hear this on occasion after a two-hour rehearsal, exclaimed to no one in particular with a glance at a wristwatch: "Over already? That was fast." Or: "Great rehearsal, Dr. Dehning." Or, best of all: "Dr. Dehning, this is so much fun."

Music to my ears. A prettier sound than a perfectly-in-tune diminished chord, or the sound that a perfectly arched basketball with perfect backspin makes as it contacts only the bottom of the net: "s-snick." Especially musical, because in rehearsal I'm no personality kid or cheerleader or evangelist preacher or stand-up comedian, though I'm not without humor.

"Alright," I hear you say, "so how does this Paragon of Paradisiacal Process do it?" "He does it," I reply, "by trying to be a good manager of the two most precious resources we have – People and Time – and by keeping my eye on the ball all of the time. It's about the music.

Through the Telescope: The Long View

Except in professional ensembles, the objective of rehearsal is not the performance *("WHAT!?!"* they yell. "Just hold on, now . . ." he says). The objectives of rehearsal are: 1) to achieve the best result in the shortest time with the least strain, vocally and generally; 2) to promote the aesthetic and personal growth of everyone in the room through increasing musical awareness and skill. That last one is the biggie, especially in educational institutions, churches, and community organizations. Rehearsing – like life – is about becoming, not being. We all make music in order to become better, more fulfilled, more interesting – and interested – human beings. Performance is a byproduct of good rehearsals; a necessary, enjoyable one, but a byproduct, nevertheless. Here are the means most good conductors use to accomplish the objectives above:

• They are masters of every detail of the score and its inherent difficulties before the first rehearsal, and they can clearly hear in their heads how they think it should go.
• They have a battle plan for the repertoire; how much time it might require, how to approach the learning of it (*Gestalt* or deductive).
• They have any necessary section rehearsals early in the term, not in moments of panic late in the game.
• They quietly command punctuality by starting on time, every time, always, no matter what, even if it's just them, the accompanist and one alto in the room, staring. They have the rehearsal order on the board, walk into the room as the second hand reaches its zenith, plunk a pitch and go. They ignore any latecomers, but get an

explanation in private, and it better be good (who do they think they are, anyway?), and they end on time, often a little early, *never* late.

- They sing a new work first, realizing that no amount of their words about a piece can say as much as the music can. And they resist the temptation to relate everything they know about the piece all at once; instead, weaving their comments about it into the fabric of successive rehearsals.

- They make the group aware of the individual's responsibility, which is to work with undivided attention and not talk when the conductor is. Yet they realize that the magnitude of their purpose – to make great music with great people – does not preclude humor and pleasure.

- They are well aware of their own individual responsibilities, which are to make every minute stimulating for everybody, teach something besides notes in every rehearsal, and not undertake too much, realizing that fewer performances or less music, well presented, strengthens both ensemble morale and audience response.

- They rehearse without the piano, and I mean "rehearse without the piano." They know that it's a mistake to assume that singing with the piano will achieve results quicker, and that the senseless pounding of voice parts on the piano, while a chorus is singing, needs to be avoided. They demonstrate for a listening chorus with the piano, but a singing chorus is on its own much of the time, even if working with an orchestral piano reduction. Some conductors, working on primarily unaccompanied music, dispense with the piano entirely and give pitches with a tuning fork instead – this is painful in September, but the growth in musicianship by May is often astounding. (After my first sabbatical, I came to the first rehearsal at Pacific in the fall, plunked a thrumming tuning fork on the table, and said, "This is the only pitch you will hear from me this year." Their eyes got big at that moment, but over the year, so did their ears.)

- They are well aware of the limitations of their own "authority" and position (see next chapter), and the group "smells" this in every move they make and in every word they say and in the way they say it.

Through the Microscope: The Short Term

I wrote the following at the request of a newsletter editor back in 1986, who asked me to write something. I would never have written it if she hadn't asked. I just took a portion of my notes, added some cutesy stuff and there it was. I no longer use it in my lectures but just make the students read it in a copied handout, cutesy stuff and all. It has been reprinted a number of times over the years by other newsletters and professional organizations so I guess it hit some resonant gong, though I wince a bit to read it now. Nevertheless, here is the message of this section of this chapter, exactly as I wrote it sixteen years ago.

Profane Commandments for the Sacred Process: Rehearsing
by William Dehning
University of the Pacific

Known as the "Twelve Commandments of St. Cecelia" as revealed to the Apostle William by several mentors and numerous years of experience;

Known also as "Dehning's Dozen" by clusters of conducting students who gather annually about the Apostle and listen with eyes clouded by bemusement, awe, or incomprehension, the which is rarely discernible:

I.   **Thou shalt know and love thy score with all thy soul and all thy mind**. You "know" it by playing it, singing it, and staring at it for hours, thereby learning it from the inside out. Recordings teach it to you from the outside in and are not the shortcut they appear to be. They are the devil in attractive packages offering an easy deal that is difficult to refuse. There is no easy path to full comprehension of a score. (Sorry.) As to "love" – if you don't love it, why are you doing it?

II.   **Thou shalt know exactly what thou wantest to accomplish in each rehearsal**. How long it will take and how it can be done? It helps to communicate these objectives to the ensemble so they have the opportunity to come along with you.

III.   **Thou shalt give a reason for stopping**. And speak to the point. Away with "let's do that again, one more time," and the like. You should know what you want to say before you stop. If you don't know, don't stop.

IV.   **Thou shalt talk only when necessary**. Your title is "conductor." So conduct. If you think you want to talk about the "cloud-like buoyancy" of a rhythm, try singing it for them – or show it. You should speak the "language of the baton" so fluently that you could conduct a rehearsal with laryngitis (yes, I've done it). If you have tried both of the above without results, then you may try "cloud-like buoyancy."

V.   **Thou shalt make certain that the "second time around" is really different** (applicable also to marriage and jobs). You have made a suggestion or a correction and they are doing it again. Did they take your suggestion or did you think you heard it because you wanted to (optimist that you must be)?

VI.   **Thou shalt admit thine own mistakes**. Do not use words to smoke screen them or blame the ensemble for them. We are not gods but many of us find it easy to forget our own mortality. Remember also: conducting is essentially a parasitic profession. Ensembles can exist without conductors; the converse is not true.

VII.   **Thou shalt not create problems; wait for them to happen**. Get these behind thee: 1) "Okay, let's start and see how far we get;" 2) "This piece (or page or line) is tough – I hope we can do it." They can if you can.

VIII.   **Thou shalt not waste time on minute details which are in inverse proportion to the total effect**. Scene at a conducting workshop of college choral conductors working with chorus and orchestra under the tutelage of a mentor: music plays, conductor conducts, things are generally okay, but altos sang an F instead of F#, basses were late on an entrance, articulation of the winds was long instead of short, and the violins were virtually swimming in a difficult 32nd-note passage. Music stops. Mentor to supplicant: "Did you like it?" Supplicant (after some pause): "Yes, well, the chorus could have exploded the final 't' a bit more . . . ." Even the gods wept.

IX.   **Thou shalt speak loudly, slowly, clearly** . . . and almost never while they are singing. This is usually futile and, to them, often maddening.

X.   **Thou shalt be schizophrenic**. With gesture, inspire, with ears, correct. One function tends to cancel out the other, so beware. In fact, avoid doing anything in rehearsal (except praising them) which you cannot do in performance: singing, snapping, clapping, stomping, yelling "shh," and such. If it were not for this commandment, your job would be much easier than theirs.

XI.   **Thou shalt make music at least once in every rehearsal**. You owe it to them. Let them know you are going to "go through it" and let mistakes happen. Their attention is greater and so is yours. We all make music so that we may have a "glimpse of the tragic stars" (Thomas Wolfe). How do they have a chance if we stop every four bars for a slip in pitch, a misplaced consonant, an error they know they made, or yet another of our finely-spun metaphors?

XII. **Thou shalt know when to quit**.   Sense the point of diminishing returns on an interval, a mood, a difficult section, a particular tone quality. Try it again at the next rehearsal. Or go stare at a big tree for a while. Better yet, let *them* go stare at a big tree for a while. Or drop it altogether. Admitting defeat is not wrong. "Plodding along in the face of certain doom" (Garrison Keillor) is wrong.

Thus ends the epistle.

It is not the intent of this scribe that these mundane laws should aspire to the immortality or import of the Beatitudes nor to that of another set of laws delivered to a grumpy leader on yet another Mount. Rather they are intended as reminders to me – and to others who would listen – that I am but a conduit for energy which is far greater than mine. No matter how great my craft or artistry becomes I will always merely serve. So will we all.

Finally, too, they are reminders that our corporate sacred process of rehearsing great musical ideas is accomplished through us by other people. (Stravinsky: "Something will always be left to the performer, bless him.") These people are at the same time intelligent, vain, kind, impatient, loving, petulant, gracious, and ignored by time, yet beloved of the gods.

As are we.

Through the Electron-Microscope: "Minute By Minute . . ."

Because the view is so close in this section, there is no order to anything, no special groupings. It occasionally has a flow to it, but often not. Some things are general in nature, some specific. Most you know, a few maybe not. I just loaded the shotgun with small buckshot for a wide spread, hoping to hit something with it. Here's a big bag of pellets, then, of what I and many other effective rehearsers do:

Spoonful of Sugar

Inject humor whenever appropriate, at your own expense, if possible; and the humor emerges from the process, not a prepared, tell-joke-here script.

Encourage as often as you can, knowing that honest praise is immeasurably helpful. The praise must be honest because the ensemble can't be fooled – it knows if it's lousy and thinks less of the conductor who cheerily says otherwise. Sometimes it's difficult to find anything at all to praise, but you'll think of something.

Efficiency

Sing for, not with, the group, (see Commandment X); if you're singing along, you can't hear as well, thereby impeding your most important rehearsal function (I know, we all have done it; I still do it now and then when the group is sight-reading, or it's near the end of a rehearsal, and I'm so tired of hearing wrong notes I just decide to sing some right ones for my own sanity. But I know it only helps me for the moment and does nothing whatever for them).

Teach principles, not cases (not, "higher on that F#, sopranos," but, "sopranos, we're in G, and F# is the leading tone. All leading tones must be sung high.").

THIS IS A BIGGIE – Rarely repeat a phrase for notes only, but only add one or two more things: *stop*-"basses, that's B, not Bb"-*demonstrates wrong and right with voice or piano*-"and sopranos, we're *legato* here, you're a bit too crisp; tenors, the vowel is [u], close it more, please. Right, then, everybody, right there, let's go." (That took eleven seconds, no one asked "where?" or, worse yet, "where we *at?*" and no pitch was given to re-start – they remembered it.)

When giving starting directions, work from General to Specific: "page 7, second system, third bar, fourth beat." I know this is obvious (a lot of these things are) but I am still capable of surprise at the number of times such a simple, logically helpful thing is forgotten or unknown. With orchestras (who don't have pages), it's "AFTER letter B (or BEFORE letter B), 1, 2, 3, 4, 5, 6 bars." They just tapped their bows on their music and are with you. Tell them which direction you're going from the reference point first. If you repeat the same passage again, all you have to say then is, "six after B," or, "six before B."

—Saying "same place" works with a chorus but isn't as safe with an orchestra, so risk it if you're feeling rich, because every second in rehearsal with a moderately paid orchestra of twenty-five players costs about three bucks of somebody's money.

—If I'm a good, non-paid singer in the chorus behind that orchestra, those wasted seconds are costing a lot more than money; they're costing you my good will. And that's something you *don't* want to spend too freely, now do you?

Corporate Involvement

Encourage the ensemble's opinion as to where people are having trouble, and why (Pitch? Rhythm? Text? My gesture? How can I help?); it's impossible to "walk in their shoes," they are inside the ensemble and you are not (these opinions should emerge in rehearsal only when asked; outside of rehearsal, they can come from anywhere at any time).

Encourage those in the ensemble to think for themselves; ensemble members of any stripe are so conditioned to being told what to do that they forsake their own creative impulses, waiting instead for the Maestro to lead them to Enlightenment. I wish I had a euro for every time I've yanked more of my scant hair out after my points haven't worked and said, "Stop. Look at the page, please. . . Now do what *you* think needs to happen here. Go." (And I don't even conduct them now.) The consequent result is, of course, delectably good.

Staving Off Boredom

Avoid a fixed, rigid pattern of rehearsal; vary it occasionally based on
the following model of a 90-minute church choir rehearsal:
1. familiar stimulant: Sunday's anthem, if brisk
2. very new or difficult material: they are still fresh
3. imminent #1
4. imminent #2
5. polish something here: this should be about 50 minutes into the
    rehearsal; it is the highpoint
6. a portion of the major work (long term)
7. very familiar or fun or inspirational or easy or something they
    worked very hard on earlier or Sunday's anthems in the
    sanctuary. Do NOT end with announcements, always with music.

Do I have to say don't just run through the pieces above, but go to the
problem spots and work on them; that the only piece simply "run" for
certain is the last, possibly the first, maybe the fifth? That if the piece
is more than five minutes long and difficult, we may not run it until
several rehearsals before performance? No? Good.

Avoid "woodshedding." As indicated above, have a number of works
in various stages of development. That way, we vary the activity
constantly (psychologists call this "stimulus variation"). This is
difficult to do in schools in the fall, so I teach them a round or canon
right away, or a very easy piece. Stimulus Variation also includes
different formations, including circles and boxes; and alternation of
standing/sitting, difficult/easy, slow/fast, soft/loud, major/minor,
sad/happy, hard work/goofing off.

Bait

When introducing a new piece, especially if long or difficult or both,
take them right to the spot you really love, or which contains the
essence of the work, or which they can technically grasp, and polish it
(!), even if for only a few bars or chords. Sell it. Show them why you
chose it. Give them an incentive to come back to it and not groan when
they see it approaching on the blackboard. This took 10-15 minutes.
This is macrocosmic Thesis-Antithesis-Synthesis in rehearsal; Thesis
is the general idea, most rehearsal is Antithesis, Synthesis approaches

performance. (I never did manage this with Thea Musgrave's *Rorate Coeli*. They thought I was nuts all year long – until the tour. Then they loved it. Until then, though, there was stony silence in the room every time it came up in the rehearsal rotation. Either I couldn't get the Thesis across, or they just needed Synthesis, who knows? Can't win 'em all.)

—Readers with training in logical processes of philosophy will know that I am not using these terms correctly. It's my idea, though, and students have found it a helpful concept; a handle on both the big and little pictures. It seems to work, so just grind your molars and tolerate it.

Speaking of a new piece, go after the *music* from the very beginning, even if sight-reading. Conduct it as it's going to be performed that first time through, even if under tempo. Show them the Thesis even if they can't yet grasp it; let them see the embryo of the Synthesis, the carrot that's leading the donkey in front of them.

Use form in rehearsal. If a piece is ABA, or A-OSS^2-A, we would naturally teach them A2 first, for example, then A1, getting one of the A's in pretty good shape. If B or OSS is difficult, I might ignore it entirely the first time through. In a rondo like Mozart's *Regina Coeli* (ABACABA), we really have it made.

When correcting, point out the difference between right and wrong and be very specific when doing it; don't just tell the tenors they were flat (aren't they always?); tell them exactly where, why, give them a solution, repeat it until it's right (or give up), put it back together. This took twenty-one seconds. This is microcosmic TAS in rehearsal. Thesis is the note on pitch, Antithesis is isolating the note and fixing it, Synthesis is putting it back with the other parts. Synthesis is always most rewarding for the ensemble (see Commandment XI). As you know, Thesis and Antithesis are my favorites. I love taking good things apart, seeing what makes them tick.

---

2 *"OSS" is my church anthem designation for Obligatory Slow Section.*

Time I: Moving the Machine

Avoid working with only one section at a time. Have at least two busy the whole time. You know how much they like Synthesis, so give them as much of it as you can, as often as you can. If minor surgery is required, see above and below; if major surgery is required, schedule a sectional.

"Pace Drill" is what I did in the preceding paragraphs: "Let's hear that note, tenors – again, higher – no, again – again? – yes." Pace Drill must be very fast, very intense and very brief, because others are waiting around. It is the only time in rehearsal that I repeat for notes only, with no other musical suggestion. As Salamunovich says, "Life is too short to just chase notes." As to Pace in general, it must be fast in American culture because entertainment is the dominant mode of the culture. Asians and Europeans will be patient, but Americans have the attention spans of gnats so we've got to keep them occupied. But they can only do hard, concentrated, intense work for about twenty minutes. Then I find that the Pace must be slowed by announcements, anecdotes, a vocalise germane to a score, or me putting my foot in my mouth. Just keep moving; a moving target is harder to hit. Speaking of Pace, watch Charlene Archibeque sometime. Whee-e-e-e-e! That woman moves. And delivers dictums like Moses on the Mount. Just as tall as Moses, too. I'm that tall but not that fast. Or Anton Armstrong. He's almost as fast as Char, and when he stops briefly he can deliver the Sermon on the Mount. I'm as fast but not as inspiring.

Handy Technical Terms

In the example above, "tenors-sing-on-pitch" was the Set, repeating for that purpose only was the Follow -Through, "yes" was Closure. If I had said, "No, still not right, we'll get it next time," then I've left the Set open, but they are at least aware of the problem and know that I am. If it's just before performance, I may say, "no, still not right, good luck." Then in performance I ignore them as that spot comes up. If it was still wrong, I do nothing but watch the altos glower. If it was right, I smile at the tenors to close the Set, and hear an alto mutter, "It's about time, pinheads."

—I learned of these terms – I was already using the concepts – plus Pace Drill, from Lawrence McQuerrey at UOP, who was working on a book about rehearsing called, *When the Music Stops*. After his death, it was finally finished by Lois Harrison, McQuerrey's successor at UOP, with the help of Granville Oldham, who was a graduate student there at the time. You could look it up.

Did you notice that I used "yes" to close the Set above? I didn't say "thank you," did I? I might exclaim, "good, great, right, huzzah, *ja genau*, there is a God," but I never say "thank you." Why? Read on.

What's In a Pronoun

Avoid "I." As in, "I want that *staccato*; I'd like more sound there; sing that for me, tenors; I want a breath there"; and my personal favorites, "don't do that to me," or, "do it for me." (I'm going to ask a rather brusque question on behalf of the ensemble – not "your" ensemble – at this point: "Who the hell are *you?*") Investigate the objective effectiveness of simple declarative sentences ("yes, there's a breath there") and the simple beauty of first-person-plural pronouns. No one will notice if you *don't* use "I," but many of your smarter ones will if you do. I know they're a minority but do you want to alienate them? I have avoided this word in rehearsal since 1966, and I am utterly convinced that substituting "us-we-our" is an overriding factor in my rehearsal effectiveness, ensemble morale, the good will of members toward each other as colleagues and me as a leader, any fun we have together, and even, praise Buddha, any great performances we may have. Comes time for performance, I don't even say, "watch me," I just say, "watch, please." See? Easy.

Think about that last one for a while.

"BE YOURSELF," Lloyd Pfautsch said. "You bet," I say, "but don't be *about* yourself."

Time II: The Driver

The two biggest time-wasters in rehearsal are the false start and the conductor talking too much. We can help with the former by ignoring the false starts of a minority that zoned-out; smiling at them as they sit up and catch up (don't take it personally, and don't expect 100% participation in the start of every Set. Ain't gonna happen unless there's a guest conductor in front of them, the unappreciative, ungrateful, fickle little snots). As to the latter, videotape a rehearsal and let it run the whole time. Then go home and put a cumulative stopwatch on the time the group is actually singing. Stop the clock if anything else is going on. Or the other way around. You need at least 75% singing. Any less, you're talking too much or something else is wasting time. Last time I did this, I excluded the break and had 12 minutes out of 100 as non-singing time. You do the math. . . Not bad, eh? Does it always go like that? Nope. Everybody has bad days and bad rehearsals. That includes the best and most glamorous among us. But at least I'm comforted by knowing that even my bad ones usually seem to be over in a hurry.

Time III: Letting the Engine Warm Up By Driving Gently

Here's a shocker for you: I don't do warm-ups in rehearsal after the initial call-back auditions. Ever. I consider them sterile in vocal development beyond a certain point; the students don't often see the reason for them and/or find them boring; they accomplish nothing toward the music; some voice teachers would just as soon we didn't (cf., Ingo Titze's article in the Journal of Singing, May/June 2000: *Choir Warm-Ups: How Effective Are They?* – not very, he concludes).

—Relative to the immediately preceding paragraph, I consider these warm-ups an immense waste of time. Our rehearsal is at 2:00, most have been awake for at least four hours, a few may have practiced, all have surely spoken, thereby buzzing those cords awake. I do occasionally devise vocal exercises which may solve a difficulty we're having in the music but it will be used when that piece comes up in rotation, rarely at the beginning unless the first piece has melisma, in which case we will exercise it *staccato* to get their bellies under the sound. I start with something quick, familiar, and light, if possible. I don't open with the Bruckner *Te Deum* but maybe part of the Haydn. We want their brains, not their bodies. Their bodies are their own business. Besides, where the brain is, the body follows ("Oops, singing now, are we? Hey!

Bod! Move it, will you?"). The music will make its own demands and the *body tends to coordinate when it knows what it has to say* (have I said that already?). The rehearsal begins and ends with music. Everything else is in the middle.

—If you rehearse before 10:00 in the morning, you should do something by way of warm-up, but get the body moving first with some easy stretching for *just* a minute or so, then running in place and/or jumping jacks and/or vigorous blubbering with the lips and/or puppy-panting, followed by some authoritative, well-supported and resonated quarterback "Hut! Hut! Huts!" Dispense with that Touchy-Feelie massage stuff, too; that just makes them want to go back to sleep or arouses them, neither of which is good. They want massages? They can go buy them.

—When they do sung exercises, listen to the exercises and coach the singers! Don't just let them sing over and over on auto-pilot, as I hear so often. Tell them what they should be doing, thinking, feeling, sounding like, and stop them if they don't. These are drills, and drills need to be coached ("pivot to the right, Dehning, the *right*, hips move first!"): "heads level, tenors – open your mouth, Chad – are you *thinking*, Brie? Doesn't look like it – loose knees and head, everyone – is that supposed to be a *tone*, basses? Do you like it? Then don't *sing* it." And so on.

If a repetition or Synthesis Set hasn't solved a problem, a common solution is to isolate its elements:

—first of all, when in doubt, slow the tempo down

—try intervals alone

—speak text in written rhythm

—take the harmonies out of rhythm, singing one chord to one slow beat; (I learned this from Kurt Suttner in Munich in the late 80's and immediately expropriated it from him.).

—Brain-Body-Breath? Are they paying attention? Maybe not?

On Our Own

—Spice your repetitions with quartets; say, "Rabi, Kelley, Joe, Yo-Soeb, would you sing that for us?" NOW they're paying attention. Every person in there is watching that score and concentrating because they may be next and they are more concerned at this point with personal pride and/or peer respect than they are with your opinion of them.

—When fairly convinced that the current problem lies with lack of attention, I even ask individuals to sing after several group attempts have ended up in the commode and I may be at wit's end for a solution: "Kirstina, you know what we're after here. Would you demonstrate it for us? . . .Great, now you, Emily? . . .Great, all sopranos . . .Great, everybody. . . ." And it is, naturally, great.

—"But you're exploiting fear," you say, "you risk damaging their self-esteem." To which I say, "Yeah? So? It wasn't fear of me, though, was it? And I think Kirstina and Emily have a nice gloss on their self-esteem right now because they did it right and everybody knew it." My only trick here, folks, is that I always choose singer(s) that I *know* will do it right first and last. The middle is for the muddlers, who will now have heard it right a couple of times.

—And I *always* choose an *individual* singer that I know will do it right. I even did this to my own daughter in the California All-State Honor Choir. I'd had it with those glazed, dazed sopranos in love only with their hair and their voices. I stopped, glared, pointed, and declaimed, *ad alta voce*, "Sing it, Meggie!" She did. And then, so did the other seventy-nine. Did they do it right in performance? No. Is that the point? No. What's the point? The altos nickered with pleasure. *That's* the point.

Teach to the best among them; hope that the others will get a glimmer and catch up; they do to. Expect the best, but anticipate the worst. Plan for success, always, but don't fear failure; it happens. I think people are basically good and want to do well. Eve gave us that choice when she went and chomped that Fuji even though God didn't think it was such a hot idea. I'll go with Eve on that one. Deep down inside of all of us is a stouter, sterner self that just needs a stiff nudge from time to time. We conductors must be willing to supply that nudge. To ourselves, too.

Backing Away

Time for some self-serving anecdotes, now, which I'm bad at in person but am becoming pretty good at it in print. Everything I've suggested in this chapter I use, with occasional lapses in memory and wits, and with some additions that I've forgotten for now or make up on the spur of the moment, as it were. After his first semester at USC, (Dr.) Buddy James, who also was singing with us in the Chamber Choir, came up to me after the course from which this book is distilled and said, "You know what I respect about you, Dr. Dehning? You practice what you preach. Or maybe, preach what you practice. Maybe both." You should know that Buddy is very talented and very smart, his folksy, legal, first name notwithstanding. You'll hear about Buddy.

Despite and maybe because of what I have said about self-abnegation, avoiding "I" and all that, I am often surprised and moved by reactions that may appear to be inspired by an opposite persona – pretensions toward profundity and wisdom; making like Maestro, playing the Great Man, and what not. Last May, Karen Schrock, third-year soprano with one more year to go, was walking with some of us back from a rehearsal in Paris. You should know that Karen is also very talented and very smart – she's a whiz in math and is doing a double major in music and *astronomy*, for God's sake. Anyway, she said, "I love Chamber Choir, Dr. Dehning. I'd do anything for Chamber Choir. I'd do anything for you."

Time Out

I think I remember having to avert my eyes for a moment. I do know I was incapable of verbal response but none was expected. It reminded me again, though, of what I said somewhere in the very beginning of this book: all this is about people and music. It also reminded me of the temporary nature of what we do. Everything is borrowed, on loan: the music, the people, all of it. How can we say, then, that it's "ours"? Do you see what I mean? There is no "I" here, there can only be "we." Buddy is gone, and then I'll blink and Karen will be, too. They are not "mine"...never were. We won't get any of them back. They all are given back to Time.

Time is borrowed, too. It doesn't come back, and it is the most valuable resource in this life or any other we might envision. Which is why we owe the Buddys and Karens the best we can offer in the rehearsal Time we have with them; why we must demonstrate by example that we respect *their* Time, and will not waste it on the trivial, the dull, our disorganization, our own egos. We say to them what Theodore Roethke said once to a poetry class: "Goodbye, dear swan shapes, turtles, I gave you my minutes, let them remain ours. It's your privilege to find me incomprehensible. The cage is open. You may go."

THEM

Bosses

When I auditioned and interviewed in April of 1972 for the position I was to hold for the next twenty years at UOP, my predecessor, Russell Bodley, was in the room as I was rehearsing the chorus, watching every move, listening to every word and sound. Bodley had been at Pacific for the past 37 years, eleven of them as dean of the Conservatory in which he worked. He was 70 years old and had been back in the classroom for quite a while following his deanship, leading the first *a cappella* choir west of the Mississippi, established in 1916. If the selection committee and I wanted it to be, I would be only its third conductor though Bodley wasn't on that committee. We were walking back to the main building after the rehearsal in that sheepshed I've already described in detail.

We walked for what was an uncomfortably long time for me, without either of us saying anything. I thought I may have bombed, tubed it, struck out, thrown up an air ball – pick your expression; you know how that goes and how it feels. Then he turned to me and this is what he said:

"Bill, don't ever become an administrator."

Not, "nice work, Bill," or, "fine rehearsal," or, "where'd they find you, anyway?" Just that one line. But what a line.

Russell Bodley knew at least two things: what it was like being a conductor and what it was like being an administrator. He saw in me, I guess, that I enjoyed being the former, was maybe good at it, would not want to be the latter, maybe even figured I'd be an abject failure at the latter – something I know with certainty three decades later. I once asked my friend, Fred Gersten, who is a voice teacher and has also been an administrator, why so many administrators of all types seemed to dislike the faculty so much. His simple answer? "We have better jobs."

As with all simple answers, it is true and not true. To compromise for

one person is to grow up; for another, to give up. WWII British Enigma codebreaker's question to young savants at Bletchley Park, England: — "Which direction do a clock's hands move?"
— *"Left to right, of course."*
— "Not if you're the clock."

As my kids learned on Sesame Street, "where you put your eyes, that's about the size of it."

Bad Ones

I've never been the clock. I do know, though, that the not-so-good administrators among Them go into their work for the wrong reasons – money, power, career, prestige; just as some of the not-so-good among Us are there for the wrong reasons – power, adulation, ego-gratification (money has never been much of a motivation for most music teachers. God knows prestige isn't). I've had *laissez faire* Bosses who tried to please everyone by taking no leadership whatsoever, allowing disputes to fester in the pack, waiting to see which of them would emerge as Alpha dogs and then throwing them bones, occasionally scratching the ears of us Betas and Omegas, otherwise ignoring us. They were out only for themselves. I've had autocratic Bosses who tried to control everything with paper, permission and punishment, and then wonder why they were the "only ones around here" with any initiative or creativity. They were out to get even with us.

Good Ones

And I had one Boss, the type of which I did not think existed, who was hired as the minister at my last church position while my family and I were on our first sabbatical in England. We sat down at our first meeting together back at home and this was his opening:

"The congregation and choir are sure happy with you. What do I have to do to keep you here?"

And you know what? I told him and he did it (no, it was not more money for me. It was enough money to pay for two tenors and two basses, so that all of us would enjoy our Thursday evenings and

Sunday mornings in a more balanced – ahem – manner). I stayed five more years and left church music forever (explanation not forthcoming). His name is Arnold Vorster. May it be forever blessed.

And you know what else? Speaking of five more years? We hired a new Dean at USC in June of 2002 and I met him for the first time two months later in August before taking this sabbatical. Again, I was not asking for more money or resources for myself or our department than we both already had. I did happen to mention that, if I wanted, I could retire forever from USC in five more years. This is what he said:

"I hope you don't."

Must be something about sabbaticals. His name is Robert Cutietta and I can sense beatification from six thousand miles away. Great portents in the wind. Can't wait to get back to work with such a Boss.

AnyOnes

Whether Us or Them, this business is about what I have mentioned again and again; people and music, mainly people. In our case, the people are those in our ensembles and classes and committees as well as our colleagues. Bosses have all of the foregoing that they are responsible to, plus *their* colleagues, staffs, and superiors. It is a stressful, often thankless job, providing not even the satisfaction we teachers and conductors have of working with young, and if not young, at least inquisitive, interested minds. I could not do their job. And I would not *want* to do it anymore than I would have wanted to take my dad's place on Omaha Beach. Or my dad would have wanted to take his Lieutenant's place: "'Sergeant' Dehning will do just fine, thank you, sir, now if you'll excuse me, I need to dig this foxhole. Artillery coming in, I think."

Thus I am deeply grateful for the administrators in churches and in schools and on the boards of community and professional choruses who *do* want to do the job for at least most of the right reasons, who don't just smirk, a la Mel Brooks, "it is *good* to be the King!"...who make certain that someone is running the store at all times, who know that consensus can't always be found and is often suspect or just plain wrong when it is found, and who understand that true leadership is lonely, even at times frightening or sad. They have earned their mansions and martinis. Mazeltov.

And I have always done my utmost to offer a few solutions to my own problems in meetings with them, to refrain from bad-mouthing the ones I don't like in front of others, especially choir members or students and colleagues. He's still my Boss. Everyone has them. He may be a bozo or a martinet, but he's *my* bozo or martinet. And everyone has to at least salute the rank, if only in gratitude for the kind people who are *willing* to wear the uniform, most especially for those who accept not only the privileges of the rank, but its obligations too.

Maestros

I've already been sniping at these folks from the distant perimeter throughout these pages, pretty accurately, if I do say so. I'm going to call up some help, now, and we can finish off this campaign. This is from *An Interview with Robert Porco*, by Jonathan Talberg, Choral Journal, December, 2000:

> "What's difficult is to prepare choruses for a conductor who might not be sympathetic to the needs of a chorus. In general, the great orchestral conductors want to do the great choral and orchestral pieces – not only Beethoven's *Ninth*, but the Verdi *Requiem* and the Beethoven *Missa solemnis*. Sure, they're all music, but the conducting requirements are not quite the same. Some people have the skill and insight to know the difference, and some don't. That is not only hard for me, but it really annoys me.

> "There's such a terrific double standard . . . You can find a *very* good choral conductor, and if he said, 'I want to do Mahler's *Fourth* next year,' the basic, most common reaction would be a snicker. However, if you took a *less*-than-good orchestral conductor and he said, 'I want to do the Verdi *Requiem*,' they would say, 'We'll get someone to prepare the chorus for you.' I find that despicable."

So do I. Hear this litany now: I don't mind preparing a chorus for *Maestro Nonfarniente* if he brings something to the chorus' appreciation of the score that I have not. I don't mind preparing a

chorus for *Maestro von Keinunterschied* if he prepares a high, soft
soprano entrance more carefully than he would for the first violins. I
don't mind preparing a chorus for *Maestro Beaucoup de Rien* if he
realizes that a chorus entering on an explosive consonant needs the
same kind of precise preparation a brass section does: they're both
"tonguing." I don't mind preparing a chorus for *Maestro Nopasanada*
if he treats the chorus with the same respect as the players, talking to
me if he hears something from the chorus he may not find pleasing at
the time. And I don't mind preparing a chorus for any of them if their
conducting technique in performance is at least as clear as mine.

I have prepared a chorus for a Maestro who did not meet any of those
requirements; it was a technically good performance in spite of him.
It got a fine review and praise from all in attendance; it wasn't even
close to being music making, though, and the chorus knew it. He did
not speak to me following the performance and I was relieved by that,
because I feared loss of my civility had he done so. The only one I
have worked with so far who has met all of the requirements, and still
does, is Helmuth Rilling. The students and I not only don't mind
preparing works for him, we *like* it, because he is courteous and he pays
equal attention to all aspects of such performances; the score, the
orchestra, the chorus, the soloists. And he makes music. Strangely
enough, he is rarely called Maestro.

That is all Mr. Porco and I have to say on this topic. You want more?
Pick up a copy of *The Maestro Myth*, by Norman Lebrecht.

Voice Teachers

This part is the last I write except for the Postface. I've been putting it
off. It is the only part of the book that I haven't anticipated with
excitement because I really am not sure what to say, or if I should or
will say anything at all – or if I do, whether it ought to be published.
I'm stuck. Blocked. The blank page looms large for the first time in
this otherwise surprisingly rewarding project. It has taken me over
fifteen minutes to write this paragraph. So I think I'll start by avoiding
the topic for the time being and aiming a deserved jab at my own
profession.

When I started my training in this work, the prevailing ethos in

American choral music was one of allowing the voice to sing, vibrato and all. This ethos was hard-won as a result of communication among choral conductors and voice teachers, many of whom worked in both arenas. It was not won without compromises and casualties of sorts in both camps, but the general agreement seemed to be that the heretofore prevailing and admired model of pure, straight-tone choral sound was not a healthy vocal approach, and gave reasonable voice teachers potent ammunition in the War Against Choral Singing. My entire career has been one devoted to depriving reasonable voice teachers of such ammunition, getting "solo" voices into ensembles and letting them sing right along with those "choral" voices, communicating as often and honestly as possible with my voice teacher colleagues, letting them hear the final product for themselves.

I have spent a lot of time in Europe listening to European choral groups, their conductors and singers. The women usually do not sing with vibrato, and sometimes the men don't either. I have talked about the resultant, perfectly in tune sound earlier in these pages. The fact is, in Europe there is still a natural, accepted dichotomy between the vocal production of the "soloist" and the "choral" singer. No one seems to mind. Everybody appears to like the way things have been going for the last five centuries or so.

Since roughly 1990, I've been hearing many American choral groups who apparently like it also. Many university ensembles, especially, are achieving a sound that would make F.M. Christiansen want to come up out of the ground and conduct. I must say that I don't honestly know what to say about this state of affairs, except that such approaches re-arm anti-choral voices in the voice-teaching profession. My wife is a pro-choral music voice teacher (she started there), and you already know how she feels about such sounds. Are we being wise in this choice of sound? Are many of us merely going along with a trend in this, the trendiest of all cultures in the world, waiting for the next one to come along? Or do we really believe in that sound and all that it implies for the voice and the music? Don't you think that I found the dissonances in Schütz's *Die mit Tränen säen,* as I just heard them sung by a German choir that won in Tolosa, to be unspeakably beautiful? And *tempting*?

And I've been talking about reasonable, rational voice teachers,

friends. What about those who are neither? Those for whom singing
in any chorus is considered to be poison for the vocal health of their
students, and whose numbers, I fear, are still legion? What can we say
about them?

Alright, I can't avoid the topic anymore.

I always find it difficult to know what to say when I encounter the
combination of Ignorance and Fear in a single human being. One of
them is bad enough, but throw both of them into one quivering soul and
you've got a more corrosive mix than h2so4.[3] Then add Power. Mix
with inert ingredients, such as Students-as-Property and/or Progeny.
Stir slowly and quietly. Distribute to *sous chefs*. Serve chilled.

Meeting Raoul

—"You know, Raoul, we have everything to gain, and
absolutely nothing to lose, by working together here."
—*"Well, I don't know about that, but I do know I can't stop
voice teachers from discouraging students from singing in
choruses."*
—"Sure you can, Raoul, here's what you say, you say, 'don't
do that.'" (He didn't.)

Parlor Talk

—"Well, Madame, I can understand how you and some of the
students might feel about choruses, I truly can. I'm willing to
concede that they may not be for everybody. I just hope that
you wouldn't discourage those who *do* enjoy them from
singing in them, whether for love or money."
—*"Oh, I'd never do that!"* (She did.)

---

3 *sulphuric acid*

—"OK, I'm sympathetic to your worries about young voices singing in choruses before they've found their individual voices and their singer's formant and their judgment. Let's put off the choral singing until the junior and senior years, then."
—*"Well, but then they have to prepare their recitals, you see."*
—"OK, then let's eliminate the choral requirement altogether."
—" . . .———. . ."

—"Look, the word on the street about us among good high school choir directors is not the best. Maybe we should do something about that, get out among them, see if we can help."
—*"Why?"*
—"Because the best young singers tend to come from the best high school programs, with happy exceptions, of course."
—*"No, they don't."*
—"Where do they come from, then?"
—*"The voice studios."*

Meeting Raoul II

—Gosh, Raoul, I'm having some real problems with the soprano production. Would you come in some time to work with them, give us some help? Maybe even just listen, see what you think?
—*Oh, well, I don't know anything about choral technique.*
—I thought I was talking about vocal technique.

—Raoul, could we maybe have lunch sometime?
—*Oh, I just don't have time for that during the week.*
—Coffee? Starbucks?
—*Oh. Well.* (We didn't.)

Yeah, I'm afraid those are real situations, transcribed especially for this document. No way I could invent something like that. And there's more, there's more – better, juicier ones, some in writing, many witnessed. I'm just weary of this. Have to quit.

Are all voice teachers so toxic, possessive, ignorant, and afraid? Of course not, most aren't. Are all choral conductors abusive of their students' time and voices in a continuing effort to adorn egos the size of Jupiter and its moons, ignorant of the voice and how it works? No. Most aren't. Aren't we all working with the same instrument, encountering the same problems, hoping for the same results? Of course, we are. Aren't there some voice teachers out there who don't equate Loud with Lovely, Big with Beautiful, Prizes with Purpose, Glory with Good, Drama with Duty? Sure. Most don't.

What can we do, then? Do I have to quote Rodney King? I thought this civil war ended thirty years ago. I really did. Do I have to tell anyone who the casualties are in this war; whose ranks are decimated by having to choose which pennant to plant? Do I have to be fatuously Liberal and say that Some of My Best Friends are Voice Teachers? That I've been married to one of the best there is for thirty-eight years, and yes, we've had our disagreements on this topic? Do I? Tell me what to do, I'll do it.

I don't know what to do.

I'm appealing to the next generation of voice teachers, choral conductors and Bosses to stop the impoverishment of innocent lives, because this generation has had its chance, maties, and "it's a bi' of a cock-up, idn' i'?"

Carry on, future Captains, carry on. Quoting Danny Glover in the *Lethal Weapon* movies, "I'm gettin' too old for dis ----." I resign my commission. Or if you like, you can drum me out of this particular Corps. Perhaps – most likely, in fact – I did not serve it at all well or with wisdom, much less distinction; that would not come as a revelation to either me or my wife.

Best of luck to you . . .

. . . Right, then.

Carry on.

US

Did you notice how much of the chapter on Process had to do with people and how little of it with music? This one is entirely about people; not much music in it at all. It is about the participants in the process – conductor and singers. It is about the leader and the led. It is about mission and morale. It is about Us.

Morale: Lonely

I mentioned "Loser's Limp" a while back. We have our version of it, too, in this business – any business I suppose. It is in politics and the military for sure – certainly in the Church (it was probably invented there). Maybe it's human, but it is unkind in any form and, well, cowardly in a leader, which is what we are.

We're unkind if we make any sort of ego-saving apology before a performance for conditions the ensemble can't control, such as not all the tenors showed up, or we had a busy week last week. (I've actually seen some conductors with big reps do this, people who are old enough to know better – they need to learn about playing the hand they're holding, need to shut up and play some poker. I once had to keep my mouth shut and play the hand when two of the five (!) sopranos were late to a collegiate choral festival. Groups drew numbers by lot for performance position. Guess which number we drew. You think those other eighteen singers weren't concerned? Did I say a word before performing?) Unkind, because we may blame our own inadequate preparation and/or poor performance on the lack of talent, attitude or brains on the part of our ensemble, poor things, who were only doing what we asked them to do. It isn't their fault they don't have enough tenors. It may not be our fault, either, but maybe if we were more gallant, trustworthy leaders – not just likeable – one of them would go out and hustle some up for us, as Melanie Heyn did with a couple baritones for Chamber Choir one fall. I don't know how gallant I am – and I've been called unfriendly more than once in my career so "likeable" may not make it either.

But all ensembles trust me to do what I say I'll do; trust that I will do my utmost for the benefit of them and the music, not the greater glory of Captain Dehning; and they trust that I will hold myself personally responsible for failure as long as they have obeyed two of my three Rehearsal Rules: be on time, pay attention. They do that, we're all in this soup together, and yes, Lieutenant, I'll take the point on this patrol myself. Might as well. I'm the first one shot at anyway.

They also trust me to get rid of anybody not pulling their weight, which in the "Y'all Come Choir" means Show Up and Sing, and in select ones means Shut Up and Sing. They don't do those two things, I usher them right out of the platoon even if reinforcements are unavailable for an impending battle. The troops appreciate that in their commanders: they lose patience with malingerers and malcontents before we do. Even if they can shoot straight.

Soldiers

Perhaps you are offended by military metaphor. My daughters and son-in-law probably are. I make no apology. I'm an amateur student of history and know that there has always been war. There are several going on as I write. I know that there will always be a warrior class and I thank them for what they do for us. Someone has to get us out of the trouble that those who run our political leaders get us into. I'm just sorry it has to be young men like my dad.

My dad was a soldier, you see. He won a Bronze Star for bravery and a Purple Heart for injury a while after surviving the second wave of landings on Omaha Beach in Normandy. His jeep got hit by a mortar round near St Lô. Cratchett the driver wasn't injured because he was drunk as a lord at the time. Loose as a goose. My dad didn't blame his injury on a drunk Cratchett, though. My dad blamed the mortar shell.

I was only in Naval ROTC for one year at UCLA because of the scholarship money (they got rid of me when I changed my major to music. Too bad, because I was really cute in dress whites. I wish I'd taken a picture). I was a mess at the time, and broke, so I dropped out of school, joined the Teamsters and went to work for mobsters and their minions on the loading docks, working the graveyard shift with drunks, near-indigents and some of the greatest black guys this white guy has ever met in his entire life. I worked for a year, saved some money, went back to school, met my wife, and with her help managed to make something of myself. (She wishes she could have seen me in dress whites, too.) Oh, and if you are offended by military *and* athletic references, perhaps you should skip this entire discussion.

Jocks

So I wasn't a soldier. I was a lot luckier than my dad and had the time, if not always the necessary equipment, to participate in team athletics, which are generally less fatal sublimations and substitutes for the real thing. They provide safer, socially acceptable outlets for that which resides in any human – I repeat, any human – the prevailing need to dominate – and the occasional urge to eliminate – another human being. But team sports can be more than that.

Anytime we have anyone depending on someone else to do what's expected of them, we have a team. My wife and I are a team: we depend on each other. The thing common to all teams is that everyone needs everyone else to do what they're supposed to do, or undesirable things can happen. The only thing that is altered from team to team is the objective: armies try to take terrain; athletic teams try to win; domestic teams try to find mutual fulfillment; business teams try to make a profit; educational and religious teams try to lead others toward self-actualization.

The one thing that should not be altered from team to team is concentration on process in the present, not outcome in the future (some business teams have forgotten this). We can only control our own actions in the present: we have no control over what others are doing now or may do in the future. Concentrate on playing the game itself, we may win; concentrate on serving the customer or making a better product, we may make a profit. Concentrate on the rehearsal, we may perform well.

I wish that more musicians had experience in team sports than apparently do. Conversely, I wish that more athletes had experience in musical ensembles. The entire society would be better off and there is no hyperbole there. The good old yin-and-yang is back. (I'm referring to "sport" in the truest, best sense; playing with skill and artistry to the best of one's ability *against worthy competitors*. There is exaltation there. I'm not referring to the moral morass that constitutes collegiate athletics at the moment, nor the egomania and greed that often seem to consume professional teams.) I loved playing sports. Playing well with a good team – even a bad one, as long as perspective is maintained – can be an uplifting, out-of-self experience. It can teach us that we don't have to be alone; that we can do things with others we might find impossible alone, in fact. It introduces us to the realization that we can get along with jerks (or worse) and those unlike us in the face of a common, desirable goal, as long as we're having fun while doing it, and as long as there is joy in the process. I try to keep that Nice Word "joy" in mind.

The Nasty Word

Team sports also teach us something about the nature of competition itself, which many musicians have difficulty with, or treat with disdain, or ignore altogether. Like it or not, they teach us some things about winning and losing and how we might handle each. I spent a number of noon hours playing pick-up basketball over the course of my twenty years of teaching at UOP in Stockton, California. There's a sign on the way out of the locker room into the gym which says, "Victory is never final; defeat is never fatal." A good thing to remember before entering the fray. Any fray. We competed to be born with four gazillion spermatozoa. We competed for grades in schools. We competed for entrance to universities. We competed for our mates against possibly better specimens (at least in my case). We compete to maintain our place in this world every morning that we roll over and put our feet on the floor one more time and go out to slay the dragon or have it scorch our behinds. You can ask Darwin, competition is here to stay. We might as well get used to it. Enjoy it even. Stress and a degree of tension are necessary for any kind of human production.

Competition also reminds us of our responsibilities to others during the process; that we can't assume others will perform our functions for us. I played City League basketball in Stockton until I was fifty years old and left for Los Angeles. The team consisted of me, two lawyers, a Pepsi truck driver, an auto mechanic, and an ex-con. The latter three were really fine players, and the auto mechanic, Graylon, was a very talented point guard who could really drive the middle. His job was to be fast and make lay-ups. John, one of the lawyers, was a former tight end at Rutgers whose knees were gone but he was huge, so his job was to be slow and clog the middle and get any rebounds back to us. The other guys did a combination of the two.

My only job was to hit the long ball from the outside because I was too skinny and too chicken to drive into the middle, didn't have enough bulk to rebound effectively, and I told everybody so. We had referees, but some of those enemy young bucks who had played in college and failed to make the Warriors were out to prove that somebody had made a mistake and they would whack you to prove it, referees be damned. Besides, I was worth more as an accurate shooter than pounded meat. More than once, I would hear an opponent yell to the man guarding me, "Don't let him shoot! Let him drive, but don't let him shoot!" They knew I'd sink that sucker. (Ah, the glory days. Sigh.)

As a team, then, we had everything necessary to compete successfully and we won more than we lost, once winning the trophy in our class. But with only six guys, four of whom were in their forties and four of whom still smoked, we *really* depended on each other to do our jobs. In one game, Graylon took one of John's rebound passes and bounded down the court. I came down just ahead of him and slid over to my outpost in one corner, twenty-two feet from the hoop. I was open. Thwap! The ball was there and I was still open. It didn't feel right, though, so I passed back to Graylon.

I mean, he took that ball, yo-yo-ed it up and down leisurely at the top of the key, and read me out: "Damn it, Bill, that's your shot! Next time I get it to you like that, you *take* it!" Embarrassed the heck out of me. Shamed me, is what he did. I didn't give him any lip back, because he was right. I didn't do my job. It didn't "feel right" because, out of some instinct, I thought I might miss and the game was close, there wasn't much time left, and I didn't want to risk losing possession of the ball. Without the threat of my outside shot, though, the defense would collapse on John and Graylon in the middle next time, making their jobs that much harder. It was my job, and mine alone, to keep that middle open for them by taking the risk and the shot, "feel right" or not. This was no time for sensitivity.

I forget whether we won or lost, but that doesn't matter, does it? What does matter, and what I do remember, is that I had let my teammates down. I had not done my job.

The Conductor's Job: The Human Part

The conductor's job, from the audition to the performance, is to help. Period. Our role on the team may be singular – many singers and players, only one conductor – but that does not mean our job is any more important than what they do, because it isn't. When we walk out on stage, *they* do the work. I don't make a peep. I need to do everything possible to help them do what they do. Any good leader knows this; great leaders have always known it because great leaders are always great teachers first. I learned this from teachers, but also from my brief military experience, a study of great commanders throughout history, from some of the fine coaches I've had as a ballplayer, and from one really fine Boss.

But it's at this point that the metaphors fail, as all metaphors inevitably must. Coaches have immense authority over their teams; commanders have life-and-death responsibility for their troops. When the opening buzzer sounds, the coach is off the floor, doesn't play; when the battle starts, most commanders are behind the line, not in the trenches. When the concert starts, though, there we are. The conductor is one of the soldiers, one of the players when the music starts, accepting applause *for* the entire ensemble when the music stops.

Morale II

Wilhelm Ehmann has a phrase for the conductor's role: *primus inter pares*, which means "first among equals," and I love the concept. It means that the group must be aware that nothing the conductor does is directed toward selfish ends or ambitions; that conductors do what they do because they love music and believe in what it can do for the human spirit. It also means that the conductor is not innately superior to any of the singers and, as a member of the group, is acting with an authority granted only by virtue of experience and/or training. There are people in the USC Chamber Choir right now who play piano better than I, who certainly sing better than I, and a few have perfect pitch so they hear better than I. So how am I musically superior? I'm not. The only contributions I can make are to teach effectively in rehearsal, guide clearly in performance, and be an empathetic leader in both capacities.

Lonely II

An effective teacher decides – alone – how to get the material across and then must judge from examinations whether he succeeded or not. The empathetic leader asks advice and opinions of those who must actually do the job, and then decides – alone – whether the advice has merit and which opinions to heed. We need distance for this. We cannot make objective decisions if we are buddies with them. We cannot be effective teachers, objective judges of their work and ours, if they call us by our first names, for instance. I do not believe in it. They may call me Dr. Dehning, Mr. Dehning, or Professor Dehning. If they are uncomfortable with any of those, a simple Your Worthy Highness will do. You salute the rank, not the man. Chad (short for Cheddar; he's Brie's brother) may call his dad Brooke and his mom Kyle, but he's not going to call me Bill. And no, my daughters don't either. It's Dad or nothing, by God, and they like it that way. I'm their father, not their chum, for the love of heaven. That's just the way it is.

Oh, but I set up the chairs if the person responsible can't be there. I often assist setting up risers because many people can't figure them out. I check lights in the hall and any orchestral arrangements on the stage myself. Why? Because I'm responsible to the ensemble. It's *my* job to see that they have everything necessary to do *theirs*. I'm there to *help* them. If there's a problem, I'm often the only one who can do anything about it. If I can't solve it, I must tell them why. In essence, I'm alone. Yes, I know, I'm *inter pares*. But I'm alone in being *primus*.

A Happy Face: Morale III

Loneliness and responsibility together impose special human duties of leadership on the conductor. The voice is the most sensitive, personal instrument there is, and the chorus, since it consists of voices and employs the Word, is the most expressive ensemble instrument there is (you can quote me). Because of this sensitivity and capacity for expression, the conductor/chorus relationship is usually closer than that of any other type of ensemble. As a result, members of the chorus know us conductors far better than we often think they do. They "read" us very well. This means that we must never display anxiety or nervousness before or during a performance, even if we're under-rehearsed and everyone knows it. And it means that we must approach every rehearsal with expectation, zest and joy, even if we are tired, sick, or depressed, because we *know* that someone in the ensemble is tired, sick, or depressed. We can't afford to be, and if we are, then we'd best be very good actors. If we feel like singing *O Solo Mio,* we'd better do it robustly.

As is often the case, I know some of these things because I've done them wrong. I once observed Paul Salamunovich come into a rehearsal and say something like, "Look, I'm not feeling very well today, would you pick up the slack and do most of the work?" They did. I tried a similar thing in one of my rehearsals some time later. Didn't work. Paul is a very special person, engenders good will no matter what he does. Most of us don't have that gift.

That's the bad news. Here's the good news. After a post-tour concert at Pacific years ago, Don DaGrade, the bassoon teacher and a monster player, said to me, "You guys are having such fun up there. The connection between you and the chorus and among the chorus is so obviously close, not only musically, but personally. We don't have anything like that in instrumental music. I envy you."

"Julia's Voice:" The Game

In a written observation report for a conducting class, Julia Tai said of my rehearsal technique, "Dr. Dehning doesn't make inspiring speeches or give pep talks or yell and get angry in rehearsal. He gets right to the music, helping us with his face and body and hands to sing it better, to show us what the music is all about and be confident when we perform. Sometimes he's funny with his face and hands." (Kissie, kissie, Julia. Your teacher gave me a copy of that and I have it in my Ego File at the office.)

As Julia is pointing out, I am no word wizard in rehearsal. I am not George Patton or Winston Churchill or Knute Rockne or Vince Lombardi or Howard Swan or Robert Shaw. Not even before a performance. I'm often not even in the room at the time. Someone else is warming them up. Then I meet them as they file onto the stage:

— "Have fun," I tell them.
— "Enjoy yourselves," I say.
— "Lookin' good, Rob," I offer.
— "Your turn to get even, basses," I jibe.

I was the coach who called the plays and set the drills, but now I get to play; now I get to be the quarterback in a no-huddle offense who's going to complete almost 100% of his passes to some talented receivers and some well-trained ones and some who are both and a few who are neither. No benches for me. No benches for anyone. Everybody plays.

Then I stand in the same place after the performance, shaking hands with as many guys and hugging as many girls as possible, getting it right most of the time. Even the post-performance debriefing at the next rehearsal is verbally terse.

— "Hey, not bad, huh? Pretty good, in fact. What did your friends say?" (Therapeutic relating of anecdotes occurs here.)
— "Well, great, ready for some Stravinsky now? Ok, back into the trenches. Let's dig some more, see what we can find."

Playing for Keeps

Only in competition does this routine vary, because competition is what it is, and because that's not mom and sis out there with scores (both kinds) and tuning forks. Only in France recently, just before walking to the Finals arena where just three other choirs remained out of twenty-five, did I do anything stereotypically jock-like. I walked up to them, said,

— "Here, I'm opening up a whole new can of Whup-Ass (Patent Pending)." I tear off the imaginary lid and toss them the open can, "Use it."

They whoop. We win.

Morale IV: Partying for Keeps

Post-game ritual in such cases is much the same as usual, but the debriefing follows immediately and involves quantities of food, Alsatian beer and/or French wine, rendering words unnecessary. Or incomprehensible. Instead we have skits and awards invented by the singers, which are always achingly funny. At least we think so. The beer and wine helps, doesn't it? There's a reason Jesus turned the water to wine in the Wedding at Cana.

Orchestras can get along without parties, choruses can't. We ignore the social factor at our peril. It doesn't have to be elaborate and it can be spread among several members of the ensemble, but the conductor must only participate, not lead, in these events. In our case, we need to cover games, skits and calisthenics on retreats, brief post-concert meetings in restaurants, and awards and skits on tours. The party on retreats is mandatory, and occurs after the campfire on the last evening before going home after breakfast in the morning. A singer may miss one of the four rehearsal sessions if fortified with a good reason acceptable to the ensemble, but no one misses the party. Period.

If a tour involves bus rides of any considerable length, one of the Social Studs or Studmuffins becomes the Bus Bitch, and is then responsible for keeping the inmates informed, in line, and entertained. For example, informed: Time to Destination? "Twenty minutes." Always. No matter the truth or who seeks it. In line: "Keep your hands to yourselves, basses. Naughty, naughty. I know what you're doing back there, Reg." Entertained. From Former Bus Bitch, Don Grube (men are qualified for this position, too, especially tenors): attach a roll of masking tape to the bus roof near the front with about two inches of tape. All must *silently* watch it sway back and forth until it finally comes free of the roof, when a mandatory, well-supported, cheer of triumph is expelled as it hits the floor. This can consume many miles/kilometers, as you might imagine. And in *silence*, lads and lassies. Sanity-saving, voice-preserving silence. There be wisdom to this weirdness.

Other Voices

Julia Tai was a voice major who also plays violin and piano very well and has perfect pitch. Thus she is now a conducting major. She's Taiwanese, and thus has to work very hard to get the good grades she does because she has to do it in English. She's here alone and misses her mom and dad and sister, though she now has a Japanese boyfriend to keep her company. She is therefore the ideal soldier/team member/ensemble singer. Who *wouldn't* want her in an ensemble?

But there are many without Julia's obvious assets who also make ideal ensemble members, who volunteer for service like my dad did, and who at first blush may not seem to be as ideal as Julia. "Walk-ons," athletic coaches call them. "Non-majors" is what we call them in music schools. "Godsend" is what I call them. I've coached and played with hundreds of them over the years; many times found them more refreshing and enjoyable than the music majors, the scholarship players. Walk-ons just want a chance to play anytime I call their number. I call it every time.

The Ultimate Team Sport: Mission

And that is one of the truly beautiful things about choral music. We can take someone who has never sung before, much less in a chorus, and give them a fulfilling, soul-expanding experience. Unforgettable, and often, to their minds and spirits, unsurpassed. Until next time. We can take these walk-ons, these inexperienced people, and after several months give them the Brahms *Requiem*. (Try the Brahms *Fourth* with a beginning clarinet player after several months. No, don't.) This is because with choral music, possibly more than any other medium, the total is *always* greater than the sum of its parts. Ask any number of those individual singers – including voice majors – to sing by themselves and they may not thrill you. But put them all into the game and get them working together and we can summon up some magic. And all it takes is "want to" and an ability to match pitch, at least eleven of the twelve. We have the largest extant body of any ensemble literature to hand them. And Brahms wrote no operas (see "Broadside" in the Appendix).

Thus the first part of our mission is great literature, lots of it, 'cause we got it. But I'm not just talking about walk-ons, non-majors, either. At USC, I often audition kids (usually sopranos) who are voice majors and have never sung in a really good chorus, much less an All-State. They usually went to one of these high-schools-of-the-arts, which often don't have choruses, they just do musicals and the like. These girls often can't read *Amazing Grace* until about nine bars in, when they recognize the tune from seven thousand movies and TV specials. One this fall had a chin wobble, for Pete's sake. (*"How old are you, dear?"* "Seventeen." *"How long have you studied voice?"* "Eight years." *"Never sung in a chorus?"* "No." I almost cried for her.) We don't just have great literature for this girl – her damaged voice really isn't ready for the best of it yet – we've also got some training in easy, free singing and some training in musicianship to offer her. Maybe if she starts thinking about right notes, rhythms, pure vowels, and phrases, that chin will loosen up. Maybe if she stops thinking about Pure Power for a moment, Beauty may become a constellation in her vocal firmament. We wish her well and will do all we can to help her with these second and third parts of our mission.

I've saved what may be the best for last: we offer The Musical Experience, the kind that has the potential to raise the hair on the backs of their young necks. That didn't happen to me as a player until I was a senior in high school. Happened almost weekly in my first decent chorus, and in retrospect it wasn't all that good a chorus, technically. Never happened in voice lessons. From what I've heard, it's somewhat rare in musical theatre of any kind. Keep in mind I'm not talking about the turbo-charged ego boost of the applause; the fact that someone *else* thought it was good. I'm talking about the fact that *we* know it's good as it happens.

Someone else liking it is a bonus; we've already bagged our booty. And we are taking it to the bank, where the principal will last a lifetime and the interest just keeps paying off, compounding by the minute. The terrain conquered is in our souls, where we have planted the regimental flag. The scoreboard says, Us-120/Us-120. We win.

ACKNOWLEDGMENTS

I acknowledge the strong influence on my writing style of Kurt Vonnegut, Lawrence Block, Richard Condon, Donald Westlake, Nelson DeMille. I have not consciously lifted anything from them except for Vonnegut's "and so on," which I use instead of "etc," but which he uses in a far more wry, fatalistic manner. I avoided his "so it goes," because he has a moral patent on it. (I knew "doodley-squat" as a boy, long before reading Vonnegut.) I was very worried about him after reading *Breakfast of Champions*, but he seems to have come through it alright. *"Poo-too-weet?"* Mr. Vonnegut.

I have been an obsessive reader most of my life (about thirty novels since May), so there are a gazillion other writers I could mention, but the breed you see before you is so mongrelized by now that further such mention would serve no real purpose. A kindred spirit in culture and style, though he doesn't know it, far richer and far more famous, a fellow shy Minnesotan only six days older than I, and a storyteller of Lutheran tales *non pareil*, is Garrison Keillor. His parody of Martin Luther's ninety-nine theses as published in *Lake Woebegon Days* is painfully funny because of its core of truth to anyone raised in that state at that time. And *Prairie Home Companion* has always made the meal preparation smoother, the yard work more tolerable, the miles shorter. *Summus quod summus*, Mr. Keillor.

I acknowledge that the names of women far outnumber the names of men in this book. That's the way my life has gone and still keeps perking along. In my family, work, and life, Women Rule. I love them all and would be far less without them. *They* could probably do with a little *less* of *me*, but I'm hanging on until they can manage to kick me loose. I hope they don't. Truth to tell, I think women should run things in general: they have more common sense, more wisdom, a more balanced perspective, greater skill with people. Most men should continue to play most of a society's games, including warfare, and many, like Larry Meredith and I, should play those games part of the time. The rest of the time, we should be housed in spacious, bright cages, supplied with books and beer or Dr. Pepper, and asked to come up with things like this book, better vehicle designs, attractive clothes that appeal to our innate male vanity, improvements in home ergonomics, interesting music and poetry, and sensible shoes that aren't ugly and don't squeak. We should invent and tinker, which are our strong suits, along with a dogged discipline. We men are not without ideas, we just lack the psychic and social wherewithal to put them to effective use. And don't think this tune is a trope on some Paean to Pacifism, either. Women are stealthy, cunning, sometimes vicious fighters. Most women are feline and grow up. Most men are canine and rarely make it past puppydom. I'm a German shepherd. ("Handsome old dog, isn't he? Just *look* at that coloring!")

Eight of those women at USC are Alice Patterson (whose name shall ever be enshrined in my Pantheon of Good, Gracious, Devilishly Capable Goddesses): Debora Huffman, Susan Benedict, Dorothy Ditmer, Myrna Kahn, Sharon Lavery, Ljiljana Grubisic, and Amanda Smith. They have made my days in Trojanland more pleasant and effective than they could ever be without them. Amazons all.

The men I acknowledge at USC are David Wilson, who is taking up a lot of slack in the department while I'm off eating anchovies and olives and washing them both down with beer (this one's for you, Dave); Morten Lauridsen, who had the most to do with my going there in the first place ("Are you *interested* or not? OK. I'll call you Monday. Sheesh!"); and (Dr.) Andrew Maz, who got me this laptop to borrow, and who rescued my wife from a month without a computer at home when ours crashed two weeks prior to my departure for Basqueland. Andrew's cage doesn't have enough light, by the way. Can you get him one with a window, Susan? Last, my friend and colleague, Thomas Somerville, deserves my gratitude for taking over much of my load at USC during my sabbatical, including conducting the USC Chamber Choir. Thanks to him, I was wheels-up with a light heart and the students are learning an immense amount from him.

Most of my teachers and professional models were men. They have already been acknowledged in the body of the book. More words here would only cheapen the contribution they have already made toward what I may have managed to enjoy and accomplish. We in the present all stand on the shoulders of a lot of people in the past, no matter who we think we are here in the present or what we think our work is worth. I'm indebted to all who were tall enough to give me a look over the fences into the possibilities of the imaginable future.

My friend Larry Meredith is a man. His book, *Life Before Death*, is the summation of his lifelong work as the Ranting Rogue of the Religious

Left for decades at UOP. His course, Religion and the Body, was a legend at that school and not just because of the title, though that helped enrollment because all the jocks and sorority girls took it, sometimes with genetically advantageous results. They came away with far more than they thought they would get going in. Larry is an East Texas Revival Tent Preacher gone bad, with a PhD in history and philosophy from *Harvard*, no less. He is in my mind when I think, when I camp, when I teach, when I write. He was always in my family's mind when we jumped into the Merced River in Yosemite, "getting the whole experience," as he put it. Larry's skills, brains, wit, zest, athleticism, and knowledge make me shrivel with inferiority. I love him anyway and he is somehow on every page of this book, though he probably wouldn't care to claim any of it, bright as he is. He will accept this acknowledgment, though, and offer me a Dr. Pepper in tribute.

I acknowledge with gratitude my publisher, Pavane Publishing, and Allan Petker, for giving me the chance to say all this in writing. I have little doubt that I may never have gotten around to it without Mr. Petker's flattering invitation to put something of mine on paper, and his flexibility regarding what that might be.

Most of all, I acknowledge the students, without whom I would have had nothing whatever to say. I am grateful to those who tolerated me, who loved me, who despised me, and still do. I am grateful to all with whom I have experienced those paramount rehearsals of discovery, revelation, surprise, despair, mastery, frustration, bumbling good luck, and downright bad or good karma. We may not have always amazed, kids, but we usually moved. I'm grateful, too, to those students who endured and exulted in those classes and lessons of insight, boredom, intimidation (both ways), humor, improvisation, confusion, a little Socratic coaxing, a little whip-cracking, and numerous sweaty, Leonine homilies delivered with absolute conviction, despite inner uncertainty (hence the sweat). We may not have always learned something, friends, but we always grew.

You betcha.

POSTFACE

I enjoyed writing this quasi-narcissistic little genre bender. Didn't expect to. Went ahead with it as kind of a tacit moral obligation to the "Ranch I Ride For" and the Boys and Girls who ride with me. It turned out to be an effort born of both conviction and love. (By the way, I didn't "author" this thing, I *wrote* it. I'm so tired of nouns becoming verbs, I could just "lay me doon an dee." Digestionize *that* one, power talkers and bureau speakers.) The bulk of it – about 70%, in fact – was written in a Spanish Basque coastal town with the Bay of Biscay twenty meters from my veranda, the water 150 meters away at low tide, 20 meters at high tide, splashing right up onto the *Paseo* at times. Surf has been low because of frequent high winds, with temperatures hovering at 65, occasionally dipping to 50 or rising to the high 70's. Yesterday was the warmest, at about 84F. It rains often here, which is why this is called "Green Spain," and it's cloudy much of the time, but being Minnesota-born I don't mind that, enjoy it, in fact. The sun shines just often enough to let me know I'm on the Iberian peninsula, which should be enough for anybody. I have written everyday here except for three, when I went shopping for family and friends in the Gascogne and the French Basque country, where it rains *every* day. My Spanish has improved; being a month in-country will do that. I've had plenty of good things to eat and have gotten plenty of sleep. Things could sure be worse.

I just thought you'd like to know all that.

Something which you already know, unless you skipped immediately here without reading anything else, is that I left a lot out of this book: group organization, program types and organization of them, fund-raising, recruiting, dealing in a politically astute way with influential colleagues, superiors and the rich, audience development, audio-visual techniques, costumes, performance logistics, dress rehearsals, recording (which, as you may have deduced, I find onerous), computer software, professional websites, even a bibliography.

A lot, really. Somebody, somewhere, though, surely has already put that stuff down so you can get at it, because it is really important stuff. I didn't omit those things because they aren't important but because I don't consider myself very good at them. And why should I let everyone take a careful look at my weaknesses? I don't want to get undressed in front of everybody, watch them laugh. Not at my age. I've already bared my soul, you'll just have to make do with that.

I've also left out three things that I *am* very good at, which are working with orchestra, the nuts and bolts of touring, and programming. I've already mentioned a number of things about the orchestra, and I'm going to leave touring to others. But I'm very good at aesthetically cohesive, unhackneyed ("Christmas Around the World!!" "Bacharach and Beyond!!") conductor–enriching, singer–satisfying, ultimately audience–pleasing programming. I try to walk the fine line between stuffy and cutesy without making the audience applaud every two and a half minutes, without seeing a post-concert, frozen grin on my colleagues' faces, or pre-concert eye rolls on the students' faces. One of my somewhat recent programming triumphs was a concert featuring double chorus music called, "Double Your Pleasure." We passed out Doublemint® gum to the audience at intermission. No kidding. Talk about pre-concert student eye rolls! But they were good sports. I wish I could put some more of these ingenious things here, but I can't.

No, I've written about the things I love and care about the most, maybe because I'm good at them. Or is it the other way around? Funny how that works. And I believe they are the things that matter the most to the majority of us in this work most of the time, which is why I have concentrated on them. Everything else is maintenance to me, not the machine or the drive itself.

Not long ago, I came out the back of our building immediately after a rehearsal just behind our Dean-at-the-time, Larry Livingston, who was also leaving:
— "Go okay?" he asked.
— "God, I love rehearsals!" I said, not answering his question. Or maybe I had.
— "Yeah, sometimes we forget that that's The Deal, huh?"

Meaning, The Deal is, we put up with everything else – with what Thomas Wolfe called the "glut and suck of living" – for that. For the messy, God-given act of re-creation. And it's worth it. Every bit of it.

If what I've put down here helps a few people or they enjoyed it, if the former and current students who love me and who asked for this still do love me, and primarily, if my wife and daughters are not embarrassed by their husband and father, their mate and sire, indeed, are still proud of their aging Leo,

Well. . .

. . .that would be just dandy.

W.D.
Zarautz, Guipúzkoa
Euskadi
31 October 2002 (Happy Birthday, Meg)

APPENDIX I

Choral Literature I – MuCM 541 – Fall Semester 2002
Thomas Somerville, visiting professor

Score Preparation Guide

The following outline provides guidelines regarding the level of score preparation for the Oregon Bach Festival Master Class in Conducting.

I. Historical context of the composition

    A. The function of music in the culture of the time

    B. The place of the composition in the composer's output

        1. When was the work composed?

        2. For what occasion was the work composed?

        3. What were the circumstances of the first performance: location, performance forces, audience?

        4. What was the stage of the composer's life and work at this time?

        5. What is the relationship of this work to the composer's other compositions?

        6. Does this composition have any special historical significance?

    C. General concepts of performance practice of the historical period

        1. Tempo

        2. Dynamics

3. Ornamentation

4. Instruments: their design and sound (natural horn; design of timpani, brass, wind, and string instruments and bows used in performances of Bach and Mozart's music; etc.); their use (options regarding use of continuo instruments, balance of instruments with solo and ensemble voices, etc.)

5. Forces generally used for the types of music you will be performing

II. Score analysis

    A. Text

        1. Biblical, liturgical, or literary source and context

        2. Literal and symbolic meaning (use of allegory, etc.)

        3. If sacred text, theological significance

        4. Poetic structure

        5. Sonic structure: use of onomatopoeia and other factors of vocal expression

    B. Structure of music

        1. Tonal structure: tonal center and significant departures from that center, variations from diatonic structure, identification of large sections of the movement or piece

        2. Melodic structure: motives (pitch and rhythmic), phrases, periods, sections

        3. Other structural matters: repetition of melodic and harmonic materials, texture, elements of orchestration and voicing, use of dance-forms, relationship of vocal or solo instrumental material to orchestral material, etc.

C. Relationship of text and music

1. Basic "affect" (*affekt*) or character of a composition, movement or section, and its implications regarding tempo, dynamics, and articulation

2. Use of musical elements (melody, harmony, dynamics, texture, orchestration, vocal range, dance-forms, etc.) to represent and interpret the text

3. Relationship of rhythm and accent of language to melodic, harmonic, and dynamic (nuance) structure of the music

4. Relationship of diction to musical articulation

III. Interpretive decisions based on historical context and score analysis

A. Tempo

B. Dynamics. NOTE: when composers give no dynamic markings or only an outline of dynamic structure, as in the baroque and classic periods, it is absolutely essential that the conductor prepare an exact concept of dynamic structure and mark it in the score.

C. Musical articulation for vocal and instrumental forces, based on textual (meaning), linguistic (diction), and musical (melodic structure) analysis

D. Balance of ensemble forces

E. Ornamentation. NOTE: in baroque and classical music, the conductor must prepare a specific realization of all ornaments—be able to notate and demonstrate [sing or play] each vocal and instrumental ornament in precise pitch and rhythm. One may modify one's interpretation in consultation with the performers, and/or in response to practical concerns of performance, and/or due to further study of the score; but a conductor must prepare a realization of each ornament and mark precise notation of the realization in the score or on score-paper prior to the first rehearsal.

IV. Determination of conducting vocabulary to communicate interpretation (including the character or mood) of the composition to the performers

A. Posture and general physical attitude

B. Baton or right-hand gestures

C. Left-hand gestures

D. Facial expression

E. Succinct verbal comments that may be used as necessary to reinforce physical attitude, gestures, and facial expression

SCORE MASTERY

The following guidelines are offered to help the conductor establish various levels of progress in preparation and mastery of a score. A conductor should set a goal of being prepared at the level of number 3 prior to the first rehearsal of a composition.

1. With the score closed and without using written notes, be able to summarize the general historical context and the text of the composition; and be able to visualize the outline of the form of the composition—movement by movement and section by section: tonal centers, general structure, meter, tempo, general character or "affect."

2. With the score open, be able to hear every detail of the music, including all the interpretive decisions you have made, while reading the score in silence.

3. With the score open, be able to hear every detail of the music in your memory, referring to the score only occasionally as a reminder of the next section to come.

4. Complete memorization of the score.

REHEARSAL PLANNING

We realize that the members of the Master Class who have been accepted as participant-conductors have considerable training and experience in planning and conducting rehearsals. Nevertheless, conductors enrolled in the Master Class in previous years have verified that, due to the unparalleled excellence of the solo, choral, and orchestral forces at the Oregon Bach Festival, it is extremely important to carefully study and utilize the following guidelines regarding priorities when rehearsing this chorus or orchestra or the full performing forces.

1. YOUR EARS ARE YOUR MOST VALUABLE CONDUCTING TOOLS IN REHEARSAL: planning on what to listen for is as important as planning what to say or how to conduct. In rehearsals, you often will find yourself so busy with gestures and cues that you suddenly realize you have not heard precisely what the musicians were playing. Prepare to concentrate on listening as you rehearse. Especially in first rehearsals of a composition, the chorus and/or orchestra will be reading the score, and they will not be able to watch your conducting as well as they will be able to watch in succeeding periods. BUT, at any rehearsal, when you stop conducting, the musicians will look up at you and expect to hear you comment on what you would like them to do to make the music better the next time. They have excellent ears, but they hear from a different perspective than you do. They will be prepared to make some corrections of their own, but at that moment they want to know what YOU heard and what YOU want them to do differently. If you have not listened in detail, your comments will be too general to be helpful to these excellent musicians. BE PREPARED TO LISTEN AS SPECIFICALLY AS POSSIBLE.

2. LISTEN FOR TECHNICAL PROBLEMS FIRST: accuracy and clarity of rhythm, attacks and releases, intonation, balance, dynamics, articulation, diction (chorus). When you stop conducting, speak to these problems first and be as specific as you can. Use the six basic technical imperatives as a basis for your first comments: LONGER, SHORTER;

FASTER, SLOWER; LOUDER, SOFTER. Is the ensemble together rhythmically? Is the continuo articulation too legato or too detached? Are the sixteenth note passages rhythmically accurate, especially after a dot or tie? Can you hear an important passage for the flutes; and if not, are the flutes playing too softly or are the other musicians playing or singing too loudly? Excellent musicians usually sing and play correct notes the first time, and usually will correct misreadings themselves on the next read-through; but you may have to comment on matters of intonation, using the other two basic technical imperatives: HIGHER, LOWER. And even outstanding musicians may not see an unexpected accidental until the conductor gently assists them (after the second reading).

3. THEN LISTEN FOR EXPRESSIVE DETAILS OF THE SINGING AND PLAYING: matters of tone quality and/or color, emphasis of certain vocal and/or instrumental lines, flexibility of tempo, further details of articulation, etc. Plan the comments you will make about expression, remembering to be concise, and also remembering that your conducting must match the interpretive decisions you have made.

4. AVOID SAYING VERY MUCH ABOUT THE MUSIC BEFORE THE FIRST READING: the musicians will not yet have heard the music, and thus will not have a context in which to place your comments. AVOID STOPPING EVERY SEVERAL MEASURES. Especially on the first reading, the musicians are hearing the work as an ensemble for the first time. They need to sing and/or play a little, and then they will be able to correct some details themselves. Plan to rehearse sections of the music, anticipating good stopping and starting points. When you do stop, limit the number of comments you make to the ensemble. As you rehearse, try to remember three important details on which you can comment when you do stop, and limit your initial comments to these three items.

5. Normally, when working with chorus and orchestra together for the first time, you already will have had some rehearsal with the chorus on the composition. **If your principal experience is as a conductor of choral ensembles, when you stop the first time, direct your first comments to the orchestra rather than to the chorus.** This procedure will help you focus your listening on the orchestra and will help to

establish an immediate rapport with the instrumentalists. If your principal experience is as a conductor of instrumental ensembles, you may wish to reverse this procedure.

6. You may need to alter your rehearsal plans as you are rehearsing a composition. However, it is important to come to each rehearsal having thought through some specific concepts:

   a) priorities regarding technical goals,
   b) priorities regarding interpretive goals,
   c) most efficient and effective way to rehearse this particular ensemble at this particular rehearsal in order to achieve these particular goals.

APPENDIX II

BROADSIDE
by
William Dehning

Definitions. A "broadside" in times past was one of two things. In advertising terms it was a sheet that could be posted to advance a commercial, political or theological cause. In naval terminology it referred to the simultaneous discharge of all guns on one side of a warship. What follows probably satisfies both meanings of the term.

The Point. The literature performed at the last three national conventions disappointed me quite a bit. In San Diego, we heard one piece by Monteverdi, for example, only six by Brahms, none by Schütz or Bach, and countless pieces of post-romantic, contemporary-cute, gimmicky fluff. One national officer described the programming as "criminal." I vowed to say something about it. Here it is.

Introduction. What are the reasons that some of the finest collegiate and semi-professional ensembles in the country present beautifully prepared programs of mediocre music to a gathering of five thousand professionals? How could so many obviously fine resources be spent on so little? (I limit this discussion to those advanced ensembles, in part because they are the ones to whom the children's and high school choirs sometimes look for leadership, and in part because the younger choruses programmed better music at the last convention). I'll posit a number of reasons that may justify such repertoire choices, the last of which is probably the heretofore unmentioned truth. I shall try to blow all of them out of the water, to continue the mariner metaphor. I may fail.

. . .Something New. We all have an obligation to program the music of our time fifty percent of the time. We owe it to our composers,

singers, and audiences. We are not obligated, however, to perform something no one knows at our national conventions merely for novelty. It is not required, especially if there is the least bit of doubt regarding the universal quality of what may be experimental or of merely local interest. Furthermore, if novelty is the goal, how many motets by Jakob Handl would be unknown or unfamiliar to the crowd—perhaps 95 percent of his oeuvre? How many Brahms secular part-songs [would sound novel]? In other words, a great deal of excellent music exists that is not familiar to the audience. And if conductors want unfamiliar, then let us have unfamiliar, but then serve us by paying equal attention to evaluating the score for its merit. Surely Jakob Handl had his bad days too, and everything that is old is not necessarily good.

...*Everyone Knows It.* You know what we forget when we give new or unfamiliar music priority over the standard repertoire? Among other things, we forget that our singers don't know what we know. Our singers haven't performed all the Bach motets, or all the Brahms motets, or all the Mozart masses. You know what else we forget? Most young conductors in attendance at our conventions haven't heard these pieces in live performance either. I, for instance, was in my first year of teaching — fresh out of graduate school — when I attended the first national convention in 1971. I heard Schütz, Distler, Mozart, and Schoenberg beautifully performed, and my ears popped open. In those days, most of this music had not been recorded, but even if it had been, no recording can substitute for hearing superb music performed live. If such a substitute exists we are either in deep trouble or we're not doing our jobs. But more about our jobs in a moment.

More important here is that so many masterpieces were written expressly for the choral medium, for us, for the instrument that we train each year, the instrument whose expression we try each year to improve. This music is our patrimony, our heritage. It is in our safekeeping, which does not mean shoving it into a museum and leaving it there. We perform it to learn from it things we and our singers did not know. This alone is reason enough to be certain that at least 50 percent of the music we program comes from this repertory. Besides, it's our job. *Balance* is our job.

Anything else is pandering, exploitation or egoism, take your pick.

...Something Borrowed. It's possible that our taste is eroding along with our attention span. Is that the reason we feel that we must present a scattered smorgasbord, forcing the audience to applaud eight times in twenty-five minutes, or feel obligated to end with a spiritual or choreographed folk-song, or—an annoying current trend—distract our professional listening audience with slides or extra-musical movement of some sort? The chorus lends itself to such extra-musical niceties better than any other ensemble medium, it's true, and I have at one time or another used them all. But I promise that an audience of ACDA professionals is capable of concentrating for twenty-five minutes on a good performance of some of the finest music ever written. In 1995, the Harvard-Radcliffe Collegium presented a program of Monteverdi and Schütz in Washington and got the most spontaneous, protracted standing ovation of the entire convention. The same thing happened in 1991 when the California Choral Company presented a program of Schütz-Frank Martin-Bach. Nobody on stage was moving in either performance except the conductor; they all just stood there and delivered the music. We don't have to sell the sizzle at our conventions. If a professional convention is not the place for the steak alone, pray where might that place be?

The Heretofore Unmentioned Truth. Programming music of the past that others might know could be viewed as a risk because they might not agree with our interpretation. Truth be told, I think this is the real reason some choose not to perform a Brahms motet at a convention. We're simply scared silly to put something up there that many may know, and not because we think that choral musicians are tired of hearing it. How could they be? I grant you it's true that, as with any other profession, we have our share of Arbiters of All That Is Right and Desirable who issue their proclamations with biblical conviction. They are the minority. Most of us are open-minded, generous, intelligent, marginally secure people who are still learning, and who feel we might gain insight from someone else's interpretation. Moreover, to be an artist *requires* risk. There is no choice in the matter—look if you like, but you have to leap. So full speed ahead, friends, and damn the torpedoes—bring on your Brahms. I can promise a willing crew at your command, and the pleasure won't be all yours.

Our Fixed Star. Choral music is maybe fourth on the social and professional music totem pole, following opera, symphony and early music, depending on which is the flavor-of-the-year. This is true despite the fact that we have a richer, more extensive repertoire than all three of the foregoing and more participants than all three put together. (Gives you pause, doesn't it?).

(Now I'm going to come about into the wind and fire from the other side).

Listen: band directors drool over our repertoire; Bach and Brahms and countless other composers didn't write any operas; orchestral conductors covet and even gleefully usurp our choral/orchestral masterpieces; the early music folks are moving in on everything from Machaut to Berlioz. I would have been ashamed had my colleagues in those other genres heard the music at our last three conventions—I'm glad they weren't there. For if we forsake the source of our greatest strength at even our professional meetings—if we strike that proud flag from our main mast—where are we, and what must we be doing at home when no one is looking? We deserve to be criticized when we fail to teach, perform and promote the masterpieces a majority of the time. A minority nod toward the experimental, world musics, the avante garde, the ephemeral, and the popular is instructive and fun. But let's steer by a fixed star and keep our sextants and our eyes trained on it, even in foul weather, so we can bring our cargo and passengers safely in. The sea is too vast and life too bloody short to do otherwise.

October 1997
(This article appeared in the December, 1997 issue of the *Choral Journal*.)

THE INDEX

Maestros, 127
Marcato, 27, 28, 100
Mahler,
    Fourth Symphony, 127
Marshall, Madeline, 65-66
Marvin, Jim, 40
McKinney, James, 58
McQuerrey, Lawrence, 118
Methodology, 44
Mission, 133, 143
Morale, 109, 118
    Lonely, 133
    Lonely II, 139
    Morale II, 138
    Morale III, 139
    Morale IV, 142
Mozart, Wolfgang, 10, 11
    Regina Coeli, 116
Musical Experience, 144

Neo-Romantic, 10-11
Noble, Weston, 96

Onset of tone, 45

Pace Drill, 117, 118
Paine, Gordon, 107
Paine, Sherrie, 107
Parties, 142
Patterns, 1, 3, 23, 24
    Home Base, 25
Performance, 103-105
Pfautsch, Lloyd, 118
Phonation, 40, 41, 44-46
Phonetics, 53, 69
Phrase, 15-16, 18, 33, 40-45, 52, 71,
    79, 87-89, 102, 1143, 138, 144
Piano(forte), 109
Pied Pipers, 20, 21
Pitch, *see also Intonation*
    Macrocosm, 75
    Microcosm, 75
Placement, 48-50, 79
Plane of activity, 25
Posture, 40, 41, 99
Precision, 3, 6, 28, 29, 52, 65, 68, 85,
    88
Preparatory, 24, 26, 27, 28, 30, 80
Primary aesthetic, 9

Primus inter pares, 138
Product, 103
Pulse, 12-13, 15-16, 24, 28, 30, 81,
    85-88

Qualifications, 1, 3, 4

Rs, 71-72
Rebound, 24-30, 69, 70, 137
Recording, 8, 9, 23, 64, 74, 102, 110,
    148

Registration, 50
Rehearsal,
    Commandments, 110-112
    Form, 116
    Objective, 108
Release, 26, 28, 70
Renaissance music, 10
Repetitions with Quartets, 120
Resonance, 40, 41, 46-49
Respiration, 41-44
Rests, 89
Rheinberger
    Cantus Missae, 18
Rhythm, pitch, 83-86
Rilling, Helmuth, 7, 8, 13, 24, 28, 78,
    128
Ring, 47
Ritard, 13, 33
Robbins, John, 3, 46
Roethke, Theodore, 123

Salamunovich, 20, 89, 91, 102, 117,
    140
Sawhill, Clarence, 46
Schrock, Karen (class of '03), 76, 122
Schütz,
    Die mit Tränen säen, 129
Seating, 55, 92-98
Second Breath Theory, 44
Set, 117
Sharping, 77, 78, 82-83
    Tension, 82
Shaw, Robert, 9, 20, 74, 83, 86, 88,
    97, 141
    Counting Technique, 86
Simmonds, Gene, 3
Sin, 33

THE AUTHOR

Writing the book on
sabbatical in Basqueland

William Dehning was Chairman of the Choral Music Department in the Thornton School of Music at the University of Southern California since 1992-2007. An award-winning ensemble under Dehning's direction, the USC Thornton Chamber Choir, won three prizes at the 1999 Gyorgi Dmitrov Choral Competition in Varna, Bulgaria, including Best Conductor and the Grand Prize. They won four prizes at the 2001 *Florilege Vocal* in Tours, France, including a shared prize for Best Renaissance Performance and the Grand Prize. The ensemble was a Finalist at the competition for the 2000 European Grand Prize of Choral Singing, held in Spain, and is a Finalist for that competition to be held in June, 2003, in France. In 1994 they were among five choruses worldwide selected to perform at the biennial World Choral Festival in Seoul, Korea. They also performed at the American Choral Directors Association (ACDA) Western Division Conventions in 1996, 2000 and 2004, as well as at National Conventions in 1997, 2001 and 2005, where they received standing ovations. In 1997 the ensemble toured Poland under the auspices of the Chopin Academy in Warsaw, and toured East Asia in 2006, with concerts in Tokyo, Taipei and Seoul. In addition to its concert and touring schedule, the ensemble frequently appeared with the Los Angeles Philharmonic and the Los Angeles Chamber Orchestras, conducted by Helmuth Rilling and Esa-Pekka Salonen. Dehning received the first annual Dean's Award for Excellence in Teaching in 2003, and in 2007 received the Thornton School highest honor, the Ramo Music Faculty Award.

As guest conductor in Europe and Asia, Dehning has had engagements with the Karlovy Vary Symphony in the Czech Republic, as well as the professional Bucheon City Chorus and National Chorus of Korea, where he has also given week-long conducting master classes. For ten years, he was the founder-conductor of the California Choral Company, a chamber chorus of professional calibre that acquired a reputation as an excellent and innovative ensemble in Europe as well as the United States. Their performance was one of the highlights of the ACDA national convention in 1991.

Prior to his appointment at USC, he was Director of Choirs at the University of the Pacific for twenty years, where he was recipient of the university's Distinguished Professor Award and its Commencement speaker in 1991. He earned his doctorate from USC with highest honors in 1971. He has done post-doctoral studies in England and Germany, and has lectured at Munich's *Hochschule für Musik*.

Dehning enjoys a reputation as one of today's more evocative, musical and versatile choral conductors, as well as a master teacher. He is noted on three continents for the profound sense of integrity and balance he brings to the craft, the musical score and the student.